ASSESSMENT AND TREATMENT OF MULTIPLE PERSONALITY AND DISSOCIATIVE DISORDERS

James P. Bloch, PhD
Bloch/Harpenau Associates
Louisville, Kentucky

Professional Resource Press
Sarasota, Florida

Paperbound Edition ISBN: 0-943158-67-2
Library of Congress Catalog Number: 91-52545

The copy editor for this book was Patricia Hammond, the managing editor was Debbie Fink, the typist/graphics coordinator was
Laurie Girsch, and the cover designer was Bill Tabler.

DEDICATION

To my wife, Jane, in gratitude for her forbearance during the writing of this work, and her continuing stimulation and support as both partner and colleague.

PRACTITIONER'S RESOURCE SERIES

SERIES EDITOR

Harold H. Smith, Jr., PhD
Smith, Sikorski-Smith, PA
Largo, Florida

CONSULTING EDITORS

William D. Anton, PhD
Director, Counseling and Wellness
University of South Florida
Tampa, Florida

Judith V. Becker, PhD
Professor of Psychiatry and Psychology
University of Arizona
Tucson, Arizona

Philip C. Boswell, PhD
Independent Practice in Clinical Psychology
Coral Gables, Florida

Florence Kaslow, PhD
Director, Florida Couples and Family Institute
West Palm Beach, Florida

Multiple Personality and Dissociative Disorders

Peter A. Keller, PhD
Chair, Department of Psychology
Mansfield University
Mansfield, Pennsylvania

R. John Wakeman, PhD
Head, Department of Clinical Psychology
Ochsner Clinic and Ochsner Foundation Hospital
New Orleans, Louisiana

PREFACE TO THE SERIES

As a publisher of books, cassettes, and continuing education programs, the Professional Resource Press (Professional Resource Exchange, Inc.) strives to provide mental health professionals with highly applied resources that can be used to enhance clinical skills and expand practical knowledge.

All of the titles in the *Practitioner's Resource Series* are designed to provide important new information on topics of vital concern to psychologists, clinical social workers, marriage and family therapists, psychiatrists, and other mental health professionals.

Although the focus and content of each book in this series will be quite different, there will be notable similarities:

1. Each title in the series will address a timely topic of critical clinical importance.
2. The target audience for each title will be practicing mental health professionals. Our authors were chosen for their ability to provide concrete "how-to-do-it" guidance to colleagues who are trying to increase their competence in dealing with complex clinical problems.
3. The information provided in these books will represent "state-of-the-art" information and techniques derived from both clinical experience and empirical research. Each of these guide books will include references and resources for those who wish to pursue more advanced study of the discussed topic.

4. The authors will provide numerous case studies, specific recommendations for practice, and the types of "nitty-gritty" details that clinicians need before they can incorporate new concepts and procedures into their practices.

We feel that one of the unique assets of the Professional Resource Press is that all of its editorial decisions are made by mental health professionals. The publisher, Larry Ritt, is a clinical psychologist and marriage and family therapist who maintains an active independent practice. The senior editor, Peter Keller, is a clinical psychologist who currently serves as chair of a psychology department and is actively involved in clinical training.

The editor of this series, Hal Smith, is a clinical psychologist in independent practice. He holds a diplomate in clinical psychology from the American Board of Professional Psychology, a diplomate in forensic psychology from the American Board of Forensic Psychology, and a diplomate in clinical neuropsychology from the American Board of Professional Neuropsychology. His specialties include clinical and forensic psychology, neuropsychology, stress management, management of chronic pain and psychophysiologic disorders, learning disabilities, interventions for spouse abusers, psychotherapy, psychodiagnostic evaluations, clinical hypnosis, and consultation.

We are also fortunate to have the services of an exceptionally well-qualified panel of consulting editors who assist in the selection and preparation of titles for this series: William D. Anton, Judith V. Becker, Philip C. Boswell, Florence Kaslow, and R. John Wakeman. Our consulting editors are all highly experienced clinicians. In addition, they have all made significant contributions to their professions as scholars, teachers, workshop leaders, researchers, and/or as authors and editors.

Lawrence G. Ritt, Publisher
Harold H. Smith, Jr., Series Editor

ABSTRACT

The dissociative disorders are a group of conditions characterized by disturbances of memory, identity, behavior, and affect. These disturbances stem from a person's use of dissociation as a defense against the disabling effects of severe and ongoing traumatization during childhood and later development. This work introduces the identification, diagnosis, assessment, and treatment of these complex presentations. It further considers problems likely to be encountered and strategies likely to be effective. Broad citation of the relevant research and the theoretical and clinical literature will enable the reader to pursue deeper and more detailed understanding of these disorders.

PREFACE TO THE BOOK

At one point in the late 1970s, a colleague informed me, with wide eyes, that he was sure that one of his psychotherapy clients had multiple personality disorder. I told him, in a gentle but confident manner, that certainly the dramatization of a hysterical or borderline person must be misleading him. I chided him for his lapse of professional skepticism and sensibility. In 1980, however, a gentleman walked into my own office presenting a story and a convoluted set of signs and symptoms that just could not be forced into the established categories of psychopathology with which I was familiar. I quickly began combing the literature, discovering the then small body of contemporary writings on multiple personality. Although this material was sparse and preliminary, it fit my client perfectly and provided valuable guidance and support for the perplexing and difficult therapy that ensued.

Since that time, the literature has grown in both size and substance at an amazing rate. A steadily increasing number of theorists, researchers, and clinicians are becoming informed about dissociative disorders and are contributing their own curiosity and insight to the growing body of knowledge. In my supervision and consultation with many mental health professionals, students, and trainees, I have observed a steady increase in the number of clients who present histories of childhood abuse and dissociative features. My own clinical practice has similarly seen the growing presence of dissociative processes in clients seeking help. Not all of these clients present the extreme characteristics of multiple personality, yet they benefit from a clinical approach founded on a focus on the dissociative nature of their experience. I have also observed a gratifying interest in dissociation among many colleagues and graduate students, themselves struggling to make sense of bewildering clients who present histories of severely traumatic and often brutal childhood experiences.

My deepest appreciation goes to my dissociative clients, who have tolerated my own learning-by-doing and the blunders that accompany that process; their courage and persistence has strengthened me in many moments of doubt. Grateful appreciation also goes to Suzanne Wade, for her years of manuscript preparation and intense interest in dissociative phenomena.

This work is intended to provide an introduction to the dissociative disorders, and cites references to the literature for those clinicians who would delve more deeply into this area of practice. The field has grown to the point that many professionals are now making discoveries simultaneously. The therapist of dissociative disorders will be developing new understandings and revelations continuously. After a while, one gets confused about whether these illuminations arose from clinical experience or from the confirming accounts of others in the burgeoning literature. I have attempted to give appropriate credit for material discussed herein, and apologize for any oversights.

J. P. B.

Louisville, KY
June, 1991

TABLE OF CONTENTS

ASSESSMENT AND TREATMENT OF MULTIPLE PERSONALITY AND DISSOCIATIVE DISORDERS

DISSOCIATION

DISSOCIATION DEFINED

Dissociation, long recognized as an ego-defense mechanism, is the process of separating, segregating, and isolating chunks of experience from each other. The dissociated information - affects, memories, impulses, cognition, perception, behavioral repertoires - then can be organized and processed in discriminable forms and manner. This strategy seeks to compartmentalize threatening, destructive, or affectively negative material and prevent it from contaminating nonthreatening material. However, the cost of this process is that dissociated material is fixated by preventing its psychological metabolism and involvement in the "synthetic function of the ego" (Kernberg, 1966) which serves to integrate mental activity via developmental elaboration.

Braun (1988a, 1988b) has identified the effects of dissociation in four major components of human experience: behavior, affect, sensation, and knowledge/thought. Dissociation can occur in any of these components, or any combination of them, resulting in a wide range of clinical presentations. In some ways, dissociation resembles the primitive defense termed "splitting," which is held to be the origin of borderline pathology. However, it has been argued that dissociation is a somewhat different process, which occurs only in response to severe trauma (Kluft, 1988a; Young, 1988). The relationship between splitting and dissocia-

1

tion will require further definition in response to increasing knowledge of pre-Oedipal personality disorders and dissociative disorders. Despite whatever differences there may be in the dynamics and developmental origins of these disorders, there are certainly similarities in their defensive functions and behavioral effects.

Dissociation leads to a more global disruption of consciousness than does repression. Whereas dissociation creates complex segregated psychological structures, repression excludes single memories, affects, and drives from consciousness without significant alteration of conscious representations.

HISTORY

E. Hilgard (1977) traces the history of the concept of dissociation to Pierre Janet in 1889, with recognition by William James in *Principles of Psychology* in 1890. Morton Prince (1906) and Boris Sidis (Sidis & Goodhart, 1905) pursued the development of the concept of dissociation, with Prince adding the term "co-conscious" to identify the splitting of consciousness in a manner different from the unconscious or subconscious (Crabtree, 1986). Ellenberger (1970) has identified reference to severe dissociative psychopathology as early as 1701. Discussion of multiple personality, the most extreme clinical form of dissociative disorder, was not uncommon during the 19th and early 20th centuries (Greaves, 1980; Putnam, 1989; Taylor & Martin, 1944).

A number of factors contributed to a decline of interest in dissociation during the mid-20th century (Putnam, 1989), including (a) the abandonment of dissociation and hypnosis by psychoanalysis, in favor of repression and free association; (b) the increasing prevalence of the diagnosis of schizophrenia, which explains several common signs of severe dissociation (e.g., auditory hallucination, passive-influence phenomena, thought blocking) as features of psychotic thought disorder; and (c) the rise of behaviorism and subsequent rejection of "mentalistic" perspectives, which discouraged the development of research and theory regarding dissociative processes (E. Hilgard, 1977). At least two generations of mental health clinicians have been taught that dissociation is an artifact of hypnosis and that dissociative disorders are extremely rare and result simply from extreme suggestibility, often in response to the therapist's dramatic flair.

Similarly, a number of factors have contributed to a resurgence of attention to dissociation and dissociative psychopathology. The renewed interest in cognitive phenomena has made research into mental events legitimate once more. E. Hilgard's (1977) framing of a "neo-dissociation" theory via the "hidden observer" research paradigm has updated the language and conceptual structure of evolving approaches to dissociation. Putnam's (1984) research into the psychophysiology of dissociation has provided empirical evidence of neurophysiological correlates of dissociative process. In recent years there has also been increased interest in hypnosis as both a method for examining dissociative process and an analogue of naturally occurring dissociation (Bliss, 1986). In the clinical arena, increased interest in post-traumatic stress disorder, borderline pathology, child abuse, sexual abuse/incest, and their sequelae has required further exploration of the highly dissociative nature of these clinical presentations. The increasing clinical detection of dissociative processes parallels growing professional awareness of these phenomena and of the high prevalence of childhood trauma, now understood to be a primary etiological factor in the formation of dissociative disorder.

A major impetus for the current clinical interest in dissociation was the acknowledgement of dissociative psychopathology in *DSM-III*, the *Diagnostic and Statistical Manual of Mental Disorders* (American Psychiatric Association, 1980), by establishing a category of dissociative disorders with diagnostic criteria. This legitimized the identification of dissociative features that otherwise would be undiagnosed or misunderstood. Beginning in 1984, annual international conferences have brought together clinicians, theoreticians, and researchers interested in multiple personality and dissociative disorder. Workshop presentations on the diagnosis and treatment of these conditions are now commonplace. There is now a professional organization (the International Society for the Study of Multiple Personality and Dissociation); its journal (*Dissociation*) provides a forum for the further development of knowledge and practice (see Appendix, pp. 85-86).

DSM-III NOSOLOGY

DSM-III-R is a revised edition of *DSM-III* (American Psychiatric Association, 1987). *DSM-III-R* lists five dissociative disorders, to be diagnosed on Axis I of the multiaxial diagnosis. *Multiple Personality Disorder* (MPD; 300.14) has two diagnostic criteria: (a) the existence of two or more "personalities or personality states" which (b) "recurrently take full control of the person's behavior." *Psychogenic Fugue* (300.13), a rare presentation, involves (a) "sudden, unexpected travel . . . with inability to recall one's past," and (b) the "assumption of a new identity (partial or complete)," when multiple personality disorder and organic disorders have been ruled out. *Psychogenic Amnesia* (300.12) consists of "an episode of sudden inability to recall important personal information that is too extensive to be explained by ordinary forgetfulness," when MPD, organic disorders, and alcohol intoxication have been ruled out. *Depersonalization Disorder* (300.60) is diagnosed when there are (a) "persistent or recurrent experiences of depersonalization," with (b) intact reality testing, and (c) "marked distress" due to the depersonalization, when other conditions known to produce depersonalization are not present. *Dissociative Disorder Not Otherwise Specified* (300.15) is the classification for primarily dissociative presentations that do not meet the criteria for other diagnoses.

Although not classified as a dissociative disorder, *Post-Traumatic Stress Disorder* (309.89) presents a number of dissociative signs and symptoms including emotional numbing, "flashbacks" of trauma revivification, intrusive thoughts and feelings, hallucinations, amnesia, and detachment. D. Spiegel (1984, 1986), Brende (1987), and others have identified the dissociative process at work in post-traumatic reaction, suggesting that MPD is best considered a post-traumatic stress disorder (PTSD). However, the argument is equally strong to consider PTSD a specific form of dissociative disorder and there is clearly a need for further nosological refinement before the relationships between various related syndromes can be understood.

Borderline Personality Disorder (301.83) can be diagnosed in about 70% of MPD cases (Horevitz & Braun, 1984) and there is considerable overlap in the behavioral symptoms of borderline pathology and dissociative disorder (Kemp, Gilbertson, & Torem, 1988). Herman and van der Kolk (1987) have argued that a high prevalence of childhood trauma has been overlooked as etiologically significant in the development of borderline personality. Many cases of MPD and dissociative disorder are obscured by the diagnosis of borderline personality when insufficient attention is paid to the presence of dissociative signs in clinical presentations characterized by emotional, behavioral and interpersonal instability, self-mutilation, and impulsivity. *Intermittent Explosive Disorder* (312.34) is defined by sporadic impulsive behaviors and is often an expression of underlying dissociative processes.

MPD serves as a superordinate diagnosis, and it is common that *DSM-III-R* criteria for a number of other Axis I and personality disorder diagnoses will be satisfied in dissociative cases. Dysthymia and other depressive disorders, anxiety and phobic disorders, sexual dysfunctions, avoidant personality disorder, psychosomatic disorders, and other conditions are often present in MPD and other dissociative clients.

THE DISSOCIATIVE CONTINUUM

Taylor and Martin (1944), E. Hilgard (1977), Greaves (1980), Beahrs (1982, 1983), Braun and Sachs (1985), and others have argued that dissociation is a continuous rather than a discrete process, ranging from normal phenomena to severe forms and degrees of dysfunction. The continuous nature of all significant psychological processes and pathologies is well established, creating a dilemma for categorical systems of diagnosis. The dimension of association - dissociation (H. Spiegel, 1963) ranges from everyday "normal" events such as daydreaming and naturally occurring trance states (e.g., "highway hypnosis," deep absorption in tasks) to MPD and fugue states which present amnesia and identity discontinuities. The severity of dissociation is the degree of cognitive, affective, and behavioral dissonance maintained within a person's psychological processes by compartmentalization of perception, memory, affects, and motivation. Such compartmentalization serves a defensive purpose. But when dissociation is developed in childhood as a "preferred" psychological protection against the damaging effects of trauma, the resulting lack of cohesion of experience and affect, and the consequent disruption of behavior, leads to a level of maladaptation and instability of functioning that is considered pathological.

J. G. Watkins (1978) and J. G. Watkins and H. H. Watkins (1981) have proposed a model of dissociation based upon the ego psychology of Paul Federn, which they have termed ego-state theory. Related to transactional analysis (Berne, 1961), which also was based upon Federn's views, this model holds that mental processes and contents are organized into schemata ("ego states") that retain some degree of inter-state separateness and discriminability despite psychological integrative processes. In the normal range of association - dissociation , these structural separations are expressed as ordinary fluctuations of mood, attitude, behavior, motivation, and perception. The more the dissociative process is used, the more divergent ego states will be manifest

5

through such disruptions as amnesia, depersonalization, derealization, multiple identities, extreme affective lability, hallucinations, and behavioral instability.

Horowitz (1987, 1988) has developed a new synthesis of psychodynamics that combines current ego psychology with cognitive/informational concepts, in which he defines "states of mind" as basic elements of experience and behavior. These states of mind are organized around undermodulated, modulated, and overmodulated forms of "emotional colorations" (specific feeling states, such as anger, sadness, joy, etc.). Each state is categorized by a particular behavioral style, self-representation, object representation, affect, pattern of defense, repertoire of behavior, and set of motivations.

In developing a method (termed "configural analysis") for studying the process of psychotherapy, Horowitz (1987) asserted that in ordinary interaction and experience, a person's various changes in experiential state are triggered by associations between current stimuli and stored information. One prominent purpose for change between particular states is to provide protection against threat. A person's shift from one state to another can be observed in their behavior and affect.

The point at which the extent of dissociation is considered pathological must be arbitrarily determined in light of the continuous nature of dissociative processes. This is similar to the problem of discriminating between personality traits and personality disorders. The presence of amnesia (although itself a continuous phenomenon presenting in various degrees) indicates a high degree of dissociative disturbance of ego function that certainly will result in behavioral dysfunction; however, many nonamnesic clients will also present impaired adaptation and significant distress.

The client's subjective experience of ego-alien affect, impulsivity, cognition/perception, and behavior defying conscious control is typical of more dysfunctional levels of dissociation. The client with a dissociative disorder will often anxiously complain of suicidal or self-mutilative impulses; disabling levels of rage, fear, panic, terror, and shame; or ego-dystonic behaviors that are foreign and baffling.

Depersonalization and derealization, common subjective features of dissociation, occur in various degrees of intensity and duration. These range from the mild and brief forms characteristically resulting from developmental or situational stress and fatigue to the incapacitating forms observed in PTSD, MPD, and psychotic reactions. These disturbances of perception usually create anxiety, which further exacerbates the client's dissociative disorientation.

There is a strong relationship between the age at which the dissociative defense is first employed and the severity of the dissociative dysfunction. The younger the child who needs to dissociate trauma or unassimilable affect, the more profound will be the effects upon subsequent ego development and functioning. MPD, the most severe and complex form of dissociative disorder, results from prepubertal trauma, and the number of alter personalities ("alters") that become elaborated appears to be related to both the severity of trauma and the age of first traumatization (Putnam, 1989). The severity and frequency of traumatization is also a major determinant of the degree and pervasiveness of dissociation; although dissociative features may result from single or infrequent traumas to children, MPD typically results from severe levels of abuse or other trauma maintained over long periods during childhood.

The severity of dissociative disorder determines the degree of identity disturbance. In fugue, a new single identity of considerable stability and complexity may develop, with amnesia for prior experience. In MPD, however, highly complex structures of identities (alters) of differing ages, genders, and personality characteristics are formed. Typically, these alters maintain an illusion of separateness from each other, even to the point of different body perceptions (e.g., "Susy" is seen by herself and other alters to be a blond 6-year-old girl, while "Brenda" is seen to be a red-haired adolescent), or the expectation by one alter that he or she can eliminate other alters and be in complete control of the body and life. In fact, the narcissistic investment in separateness that alters maintain is an impediment to the therapeutic process, which seeks to reduce the degree of reliance upon the dissociative process and to develop an integration of psychological function and identity.

Although the clinician is best served by thinking in terms of the dissociative continuum rather than in terms of discrete diagnostic categories, it is clearly useful to discriminate between major dissociative conditions. The two conditions to be discussed here are MPD and ego-state disorder (a broad category that subsumes a wide variety of dissociative phenomena). A brief discussion of the dissociative aspects of borderline personality will follow.

Multiple Personality Disorder (MPD). MPD is characterized by the simultaneous presence of two or more complex ego organizations (alters) within a person, each with its own sense of identity. These alters co-exist in consciousness in complex relationship to each other, most often with alternation of executive control over motor behavior and dominance of consciousness. Typically, there is a "host" personality who serves as the personality system's ambassador to the interpersonal world, and a variety of alters who "come out" only at certain times or in response to particular events and stimuli. Often the host is amnesic to the presence of the alters, and is bewildered by the time discontinuity created by amnesia for those times when other alters were executive (referred to as "losing time"), as well as by the manifestations of the other alters' actions. Sometimes the host will complain of auditory hallucinations (alters communicating orally), which can lead to the misdiagnosis of schizophrenia or hallucinosis.

Kluft (1987a) noted that MPD does not present in a clear and consistent manner; instead, "windows of diagnosability" occur during which dissociative symptoms can be observed by an alert clinician. It has been found that the average MPD client receives professional mental health services for more than 6 years prior to correct diagnosis, reflecting a combination of clinician error and variability in the presentation of dissociative signs and symptoms (Putnam et al., 1986). The MPD system of alters generally seeks to avoid detection (Kluft, 1985b), with fewer than 10% of true MPD cases presenting in a histrionic, florid manner which intentionally draws attention to the existence of alters. Although some cases come to professional attention during a period of crisis involving severe dissociative disorganization of affect or behavior, the more typical pattern is the gradual disclosure and manifestation of dissociation over the course of the MPD client's involvement in a supportive and consistent therapeutic relationship with a competent professional psychotherapist. At least some alters other than the host are quite aware of the true nature of the condition and inform the therapist of the dissociative condition only after determining that there is sufficient safety in the treatment relationship to justify the vulnerability that the system experiences once the secret of MPD is divulged.

One characteristic MPD shares with borderline personality is the frequent presentation of extreme unmodulated affects, impulses, and motivations. Both the splitting defense and the dissociative defense prevent normal neutralization of affect, thereby causing internal states of arousal to be intense and poorly controlled. Many alters in MPD therefore present acute distress, ambivalence, acting out, and inconsistent or contradictory behaviors.

Other aspects of MPD will be discussed in later sections.

Ego-State Disorder (ESD). J. G. Watkins (1978) and J. G. Watkins and H. H. Watkins (1979) have described the disordered ego-state structure of personality as leading to "covert multiple personality," in which conflicts among ego states can create intense dysfunction that is less severe than MPD. Ego-state disorders (ESD) are different from MPD in that dissociative barriers are less fully elaborated (resulting in less identity disturbance), the client presents less amnesia and disturbance of consciousness, and the client manifests covert rather than overt inter-state conflicts. Whereas MPD alters alternate executive control (switch) spontaneously, the switch process in ESD requires facilitation by hypnosis or various therapeutic enactments that heighten the discrimination between ego states (e.g., two-chair work, imagery techniques). Similarly, although MPD alters typically experience themselves as persons distinctly different from each other, ESD ego states tend to experience themselves as "parts" of one person. The degree of dissociation is the degree to which a person defines various self-stimuli (affect, cognition, impulse, identity, behavior, memory, motivation) as "not-me," ranging from the relatively complete disowning of self-characteristics in MPD to the milder and less disruptive exclusions in ESD. This is a phenomenological distinction, seldom directly related to objectively defined clinical signs.

Since ESD is defined structurally and relatively, rather than behaviorally and absolutely, this area of dysfunction does not correspond to the descriptive categorical nosology of the *DSM-III-R*. The best fit would be the *DSM-III-R* category of *Dissociative Disorder Not Otherwise Specified* (300.15). Many ESD clients satisfy other Axis I and Axis II diagnostic criteria, based upon behavioral symptoms including impulsivity, affective distress and instability, somatoform dysfunction, eating disorder, substance abuse, post-trauma reaction, sexual dysfunction, and atypical behaviors.

In addition to the conflict between ego states that leads to the client's distress and dysfunction, ego states present their own distresses and dysfunctional behaviors. The unmodulated affect and impulse characteristic of MPD and borderline personality is also found in ESD, due to a failure to neutralize affect resulting

9

from experiences in childhood and adolescence. Perception and appraisal/attributional processes are generally distorted and each ego state maintains a somewhat idiosyncratic and discriminable perspective, self-representation, and object representation/world-view. This is because dissociation prevents the synthesis of accurate representations of experience. Child and adolescent ego states in adult ESD clients have been fixated in development, usually due to some degree of trauma, and exhibit the style of cognition, emotionality, and behavior characteristic of their developmental level. Dissociation causes the maintenance over time of grossly inconsistent and often contradictory patterns of experience within a single person, thereby constituting an intrapsychic system of parts that exist in complex interrelationships.

The popularity of the concept of the "inner child" (Abrams, 1990) is growing. The current attention to the problems of adult survivors of dysfunctional families (Missildine, 1963; Whitfield, 1987) and of incest or other sexual abuse (Bass & Davis, 1988; Briere, 1989; Courtois, 1988) has led to greater professional and public awareness of a particularly common ego-state presentation: a child ego state (originating in traumatic, shame-inducing, or otherwise disaffirming circumstances) that maintains the original experience and position unchanged as the person otherwise continues to mature and develop into a relatively functional adult. Any event or experience that presents a child with threatening or unassimilable information is a possible precipitant of the dissociation of an ego state. Bowlby (1980) noted that parental denial of their child's experience results in the child's relegation of the internal representation of that experience to the unconscious. It appears that repeated reliance upon this excluding type of defensive maneuver during the prepubertal period of neural and psychological plasticity can lead to a gradual and progressive elaboration of separate ego states that remain co-conscious and engage in parallel processing of sensory input and mental activity.

Gestalt therapy (E. Polster & M. Polster, 1973) emphasizes the identification of "polarities," essentially dialectical ego states that present opposing motivations and characteristics in a conflictual and disruptive manner. The accentuation of these opposing states via two-chair work, dream work, and other forms of enactment is a major therapeutic activity. The goal of these activities is to increase acceptance of those aspects of self that have previously been dissociated and rejected, and to resolve those conflicts to the greatest degree possible. Psychosynthesis (Assagioli, 1965) refers to ego states as "subpersonalities" and focuses upon identifying and resolving the conflicts between these subpersonalities. Transactional analysis (TA) is a model of understanding human behavior and of psychotherapy built upon the natural, nonpathological existence of ego states (Berne, 1961). TA tends to emphasize working on interpersonal transaction problems in group therapy more than intrapersonal conflict. However, when combined with gestalt therapy principles, as is often the case in clinical practice, this approach addresses ego-state problems quite directly.

Self-psychology (Kohut, 1971) and object-relations theory (Kernberg, 1966) address the development of ego-state structures in their own terminologies. As will be discussed more fully later, the ego-state therapy of John and Helen Watkins (J. G. Watkins, 1978; J. G. Watkins & H. H. Watkins, 1979) is based upon the identification and resolution of ego-state conflicts that create pathological symptoms and distress and uses an eclectic mix of techniques that include education, hypnosis, enactment, and conflict mediation to produce inter-state compromise and cooperation.

Rowan (1990) provides a thorough discussion of the concept of subpersonality as considered by various personality theorists and clinicians. His phenomenological account discusses the nature and origins of part-self structures and presents research findings that support and illuminate this perspective.

Thus, the part-self nature of personality and human behavior is acknowledged by a number of different theories and therapeutic approaches. The general public also typically finds an ego-state perspective congruent with their subjective experiences. Therefore, this perspective is generally useful in comprehending and explaining the complexities of psychological events, even to those not well-versed in psychological concepts.

Borderline Personality. Although borderline pathology is frequently identified by mental health professionals, its treatment remains difficult and lengthy. As Beahrs (1982) and others have observed, the majority of borderline clients present personality structures of sufficient complexity and stability over time that they can be usefully considered as dissociative disorders of the ego-state disorder type. It would be naïve to expect a simple and rapid approach to the psychotherapy of psychopathology that so profoundly influences personality development; however, an ego-state formulation of borderline cases often can facilitate the clinician's understanding of otherwise perplexing phenomena and the client's therapeutic movement toward greater psychological integration.

DISSOCIATION AS A RESPONSE TO TRAUMA

Etiology of MPD. Kluft (1986b) has defined four factors that lead to the development of MPD: (a) a hypothesized biological capacity to dissociate, (b) repeated traumatic experience in childhood, (c) shaping influences that consolidate dissociated psychological processes into relatively well-formed alters, and (d) inadequate supports and protection to restore normal integrative processes of personality development. Braun and Sachs (1985) similarly identify repeated traumatization (usually including severe physical abuse, sexual abuse, or incest) as a precipitating factor in the causation of MPD. Putnam et al. (1986) found that 97% of a highly representative clinical sample of 100 diagnosed MPD patients had experienced severe childhood abuse, with 83% reporting sexual abuse, 68% reporting incest, and 68% reporting a combination of physical and sexual abuse; 45% of this sample also reported witnessing a violent death in childhood. Coons and Milstein (1984) found that 85% of their sample of 20 MPD patients presented histories of child abuse, with 75% reporting sexual abuse and 50% reporting physical abuse. As Putnam (1989) stated, most MPD clients have been subjected to multiple instances and forms of childhood trauma. Although reliable estimates are not available, it appears that a significant subgroup of MPD clients were subjected in childhood to ritualistic abuse by cult groups.

These statistics and the mention of cult victimization may seem unbelievable to the skeptical reader. The frequency and severity of child abuse and incest is only recently gaining professional and public awareness, and the phenomena of satanic cult activities and ritualistic abuse are still largely unrecognized except by law enforcement personnel and clinicians specializing in the treatment of MPD and dissociative disorder. These cult groups maintain secrecy by intimidation and coercion, avoid public visibility, and command strong loyalty among members. Clinicians should not be surprised to encounter dissociative clients who have suffered actual ritualistic abuse and should not dismiss reports of such abuse as improbable. The prevalence of ritualistic abuse in the development of MPD continues to inspire controversy among the members of the International Society for the Study of Multiple Personality and Dissociation (see Appendix, pp. 85-86).

Summit (1983) and Goodwin (1985) have identified the role of professional incredulity in the face of disclosure of child abuse as a defense against accepting the existence of severe brutality in the lives of clients. The clinician working with victims and adult survivors of sadistic abuse, sexual abuse, and incest is regularly exposed to vivid accounts of severely traumatizing events perpetrated by parents and other adult caretakers. Often, he or she experiences intense emotional reactions to these reports and the obvious destructive effects of these experiences.

When repeated child abuse and trauma stems from the abusive behavior of parents or others upon whom the child depends for security and attachment, a pervasive distrust of relationships and a deep sense of shame develops that severely impairs self-esteem and interpersonal functioning. The abused child's experience of life generates complex representations and expectancies which severely limit and determine later development and adaptive competence. Particularly when the child has been subjected to extremely inconsistent or contradictory experiences such as parental vacillation between abuse and indulgence or affirmation, it is likely that dissociated structures of self-representation, object representation, and affect will develop in order to accommodate severely discrepant information. Over time, these structures separately coalesce, become fixed, and are elaborated into complex forms of alters and ego states.

Dissociation is an efficient defense. It performs a variety of functions, including (a) the encapsulation of the memory and affect of trauma, (b) the containment of unacceptable or risky impulses (particularly aggression, suicidality, and sexuality), (c) the accommodation of extremely discrepant affect and information, (d) the protection of "secrets" from disclosure, (e) the containment of "toxic introjects" that develop in response to brutality by primary attachment figures, and (f) the development of specialized adaptive competencies that otherwise would be inhibited by traumatic experience (Bloch, 1988). Once the child successfully employs the dissociative defense, dissociation becomes the preferred defensive process and often will be used subsequently even when less extreme defense processes might suffice in threat containment.

13

Post-Traumatic Stress Disorder (PTSD). The severity of dissociation in a particular case of PTSD is related to the developmental level of the traumatized person at the time of initial traumatization, as well as the severity and frequency of trauma. Traumatization occurring only after consolidation of a relatively cohesive and integrated personality structure may result in dissociative symptoms including amnesia, but will not tend to lead to the establishment of complex alters and ego states. The adult-onset PTSD client may manifest undermodulated states of rage, panic, generalized distress, and intense impulsivity. However, these presentations still involve a level of structural integration of self-representation and object-representation that is superior to that of MPD and borderline clients. The traumatic revivification known as "flashback" and the intrusion of trauma-related cognitive/affective material into the flow of consciousness are consequences of the permeability of repressive and dissociative barriers. The emotional "numbing" characteristic of PTSD is a dissociative anesthetic response which is also common in MPD.

"BELIEF" VERSUS SKEPTICISM

Skepticism about the very existence and nature of this form of disturbance is strong and influential in determining clinical care in the area of MPD and dissociative disorder. This skepticism can certainly be attributed in part to the fact that only recently has the development of an adequate knowledge base regarding child abuse, incest, post-trauma phenomena, hypnosis, ego development, and cognitive psychology occurred to support including this area of clinical practice in educational curricula.

Another factor is the antipathy that many people feel toward the extreme, intense, and disruptive behavior typically generated by the dissociative process. Mental health professionals, many already reeling from the demands imposed by the treatment of borderline clients, are understandably reluctant to engage in the complex and extensive diagnostic formulations and treatment processes that these disorders require. The very idea that a number of separate identities or personalities that engage in complicated and often seemingly bizarre behaviors can exist within an individual is preposterous to many clinicians. These practitioners develop an acceptance of these phenomena only after actually encountering a dissociative disorder in their clinical practice and becoming perplexed and confused. Only then will they review the growing body of professional literature or attend training in this area.

Most clinicians treating MPD learn of the considerable damage and inadvertent mistreatment experienced by MPD clients that is attributable to misdiagnosis, an inevitable result of extreme skepticism by professionals.

One should maintain a cautious and conservative stance toward MPD in forensic settings (Kluft, 1987b) in order to minimize the costs inherent in "false positive" diagnostic errors. In the treatment setting, however, the greater cost occurs when professional ignorance of dissociative phenomena leads to "false negative" errors, which result in ineffective or harmful treatment. The clinician new to this area of practice should be careful not to let enthusiasm and fascination with dissociation turn into finding every case to be MPD; however, when the client's presentation includes features characteristic of dissociative disorder or inconsistent with other known disorders, one should carefully attempt to rule out MPD or other dissociative dysfunction.

To some degree, the intensity of professional rejection and ignorance of dissociative disorder can be reduced by emphasizing the wide range of dissociative phenomena (the dissociative continuum) rather than the extreme forms found in MPD. Many commonly accepted clinical presentations have dissociative features as central aspects. Clinicians incredulous about the simultaneous existence of multiple identities within an individual may be able to appreciate the less dramatic instances of dissociative defense. What mental health professional has not encountered severe intrapsychic conflict and its disruptive effects, ego-dystonic behavior, or suicidal impulse that frightens the client? These and other common clinical problems can best be understood through a comprehension of dissociation, which may then allow for acceptance of the more florid forms of dissociation if they are actually encountered.

Perhaps the most fascinating facet of dissociation lies in the multiplicity of identity unique to MPD. It is this aspect which best illuminates the constructive and representational nature of personality, challenging the "one body, one mind" premise underlying western conceptions of personhood. By understanding the complex etiology and characteristics of MPD, we learn more about the ways in which each person forms a self and a way to comprehend his or her experiences.

CLINICAL PRESENTATION OF
MPD AND DISSOCIATIVE DISORDER

CLINICAL SIGNS AND SYMPTOMS

Seldom do MPD and dissociative disorder present clearly and unequivocally, and seldom are these conditions detected upon initial clinical evaluation. The majority of these clients attempt to conceal the dissociative aspect of their dysfunction. The "host" personality (usually the presenting alter) is often unaware of the nature of the problem, serves as a poor informant and offers vague, incomplete, and baffling information when interviewed.

Kluft (1985b) reports that approximately 40% of MPD clients show no signs of MPD initially and are identified only via ancillary information or by alters directly alerting the clinician to their presence and the nature of the dissociative dysfunction after some time in treatment. Another 40% display subtle signs of dissociation that an alert and informed clinician can identify, and about 15% are identified when spontaneous dissociation occurs in a session.

The client who has previously received and accepted an accurate diagnosis of MPD may inform the clinician of the diagnosis and openly discuss various aspects of the disorder and prior treatment. However, most clients present with focal symptoms including depression, anxiety, panic, confusion, phobia, dysfunctional behavior (impulsivity, acting out, abusiveness, explosiveness, borderline instability, self-mutilation, suicidality, promiscuity, compulsivity), substance abuse or chemical dependency, amnesia, ego-dystonic impulses, psychosomatic complaints, headaches, conversion disorder, disturbing imagery or memory recall, "flashbacks" of traumatic experiences, depersonalization, hallucinations (primarily auditory, but occasionally visual), and eating disorders.

In contrast to the relative lack of concern of the hysteric experiencing dissociative disturbances, MPD and ESD clients tend to present considerable anxiety, apprehension, agitation, and bewilderment regarding behavioral and conversion symptoms, amnesia, and other anomalies. The clinician often will note a compensatory compulsive preoccupation with loss of control of affect, cognition, and behavior.

The vast majority of dissociative clients presenting in mental health settings are female. However, mental health professionals working in correctional settings observe considerable dissociative disturbance, much of which is undiagnosed, in male offenders. Female dissociators are more likely to present distress symptoms and nonaggressive behavioral disturbances, while males are more likely to present antisocial or aggressive acting-out behaviors (Putnam, 1989).

Depression, the most common focal presentation of MPD clients, may range from psychotic intensity to moderate or mild chronic dysthymia. The host personality is typically demoralized, voices helplessness, hopelessness, and bewilderment, and feels ineffectual in daily living. Often the host will report sporadic intensification of depression, attributable to breakthrough affect from a more severely depressed alter/ego state. This may be accompanied by suicidal impulses which frighten the host, cannot be explained by the host, and have no immediately determinable cognitive or situational referents. Some alters are formed specifically to contain depressive affect and perspectives that arise from the client's life experiences; trauma-repository alters tend to be existentially depressed in response to repeated brutalization, rejection, or humiliation at the hands of primary attachment figures.

Generally, anxiety and panic are manifestations in the host of variable levels of threat resulting from the affect and impulses of various alters, reminiscent of the classical view of neurotic anxiety. Perceptual hypervigilance and autonomic hyperreactivity are common, with psychosomatic symptoms often resulting from chronic autonomic arousal. Trauma-repository alters and child alters/ego states tend to display a sense of being overwhelmed by historical and contemporaneous events, since they lack the ego strength and compensatory adaptiveness to adjust to the demands of daily living. Diffuse intense terror will frequently be noted, due to association of current stimuli with traumatic experience. Some MPD clients present focal phobias which initially may have no comprehensible origin, but eventually will be seen to be associated with specific traumatic events.

Behavioral acting out is a common feature of MPD and ESD clients. The undermodulated affects and impulses of alters/ego states often will be expressed in volatile explosiveness, intense anger, recurrent suicidality, and impulsive ego-dystonic behavior which the host finds perplexing and quite embarrassing. In fact, the uncharacteristic nature of this behavior is often the first clue the clinician has regarding the dissociative nature of the client (e.g., a shy, avoidant male who sporadically explodes into aggressive behavior; a compulsive, conforming person who on occasion writes bad checks or behaves in a narcissistic, sociopathic manner; a prim and sexually constricted woman who regularly engages in promiscuous sexual behavior). In dissociative clients with histories of severe early sexual abuse by primary attachment figures, one or more promiscuous or highly sexualized alters/ego states will frequently exist, sometimes engaging in prostitution.

Substance abuse and chemical dependency often conceal dissociative dysfunction, and "blackouts" attributed to alcohol intoxication sometimes are the amnesic episodes of MPD, particularly when no alcohol has been consumed. Host personalities and other alters/ego states tend to use alcohol and illicit and prescription drugs, particularly CNS depressants, as self-medication to manage intense distress. Antisocial and narcissistic alters/ego states may prefer CNS stimulants to bolster their confidence, energy, and stimulation level, and choose alcohol and other depressants for the disinhibition of controls over impulses and acting out. Frequently an acting-out alter/ego state will use alcohol to suppress the host and gain executive status in order to pursue gratification without interference.

The cardinal feature of MPD is found in the dissociative symptom of amnesia ("lost time," "blackouts"), both for lengthy periods of childhood or later life during which severe trauma was suffered and for current periods during which various alters are executive and the host and other alters are not conscious. These periods of "lost time" vary in duration from minutes to months - and in some cases, years - during which the executive alter may be acting out or pursuing goals unique to that alter. Host personalities are often alarmed when they regain consciousness in unfamiliar locations (e.g., cities hundreds of miles from home) with no awareness of travel or intervening behaviors. ESD clients will often report amnesia for various periods of childhood, but will not experience clear contemporaneous amnesia.

This recurrent loss of awareness prevents the development of experiential continuity and a stable sense of time and sequence. MPD clients frequently experience confusion regarding cause-and-effect relationships and the sequencing of events, including confusion regarding their own histories and current experience. Some alters remain undisturbed by this disruption because they are conscious at all times, even when not executive.

Other dissociative symptoms common in the clinical presentation of MPD and ESD are depersonalization and derealization, alterations in the normal subjective experience of self and events.

18

Depersonalization is a disruption of one's sense of identity, creating an estrangement from the familiar feeling of being oneself, while derealization is a sense of the unreality of one's experience. These disturbances of subjective reality must be evaluated carefully, for they can indicate either minor dissociation, severe dissociation, or imminent psychotic decompensation.

"Flashbacks," revivifications of traumatic experiences, occur spontaneously in some cases of MPD prior to the initiation of appropriate psychotherapy, due to a failure of dissociative defenses to contain the affect and memory of trauma. These revivifications will occur more frequently after treatment begins and the abreactive process begins. These phenomena will be discussed in more detail later.

Hallucinations are common in MPD. Auditory hallucinations are the internalized voices of alters or the auditory revivifications of the voices of significant others. Visual hallucinations are typically revivifications of traumatic experience or images created by an alter. MPD clients are generally reluctant to acknowledge hallucinatory experiences because they are convinced that these experiences are proof of "craziness." Once disclosed, these hallucinatory symptoms all too often lead to misdiagnosis and inappropriate treatment with antipsychotic medication.

Varied and often shifting psychosomatic symptoms are common in MPD and ESD. Severe unremitting headaches are a frequent complaint, often indicating conflict between the host and alters for executive control and emotional dominance, or serving as a somatization of the acute distress of an alter. In some situations, an acting-out alter will "give a headache" to the host or another alter as an act of harassment.

The MPD client will often complain of pain or recurrent sensation (e.g., choking, pressure) for which no physical cause can be found. This is discovered to be a "physical memory," a somatic revivification of pain experienced during traumatic experience. These symptoms tend to occur most commonly prior to abreactive episodes during therapy, but may be observed whenever dissociative defenses are weakened by stress or trauma-triggering stimuli. This pain is often localized to areas of sexual abuse (e.g., genitals and abdominal areas), but may also be experienced at the bodily site of other abuse (e.g., cigarette burns, beatings, binding, etc.).

Other psychosomatic symptoms include numbness, tingling sensations, visual disturbances, loss of consciousness, and muscular weakness. Putnam (1989) cites several research studies identifying a considerable range and significant incidence of psycho-somatic presentations in MPD, including psychogenic blindness and deafness. Psychogenic muteness of an alter typically stems from severe trauma or from the alter's preverbal developmental level and serves to prevent disclosure of "secrets" about abuse. A variety of cardiac, respiratory, and gastrointestinal disturbances are common, including palpitations, chest pain, ulcer, and intestinal dysfunction. Putnam et al. (1986) found a significant incidence of eating disorders in MPD cases, and Torem (1986) has identified eating disorders as a manifestation of ESD. In these situations, the dysfunctional eating behavior will have a dynamic meaning (e.g., obesity to dissuade sexual advances, anorexia as a repetition of disturbed feeding or food withholding in childhood or to prevent growing up, etc.), or will be the manifestation of inter-alter/ego-state conflict.

The preceding discussion of symptoms associated with MPD and ESD indicates one of the major problems of diagnosis. Apart from amnesia, there is no single symptom or set of symptoms unique to these disorders. In the absence of an alter switch early in the evaluation, the clinician will find no quick, simple, or clear resolution to these diagnostic problems. The presence of a complex symptom picture with sporadic, variable, and atypical symptom patterns and an atypical or paradoxical response to the treatment of specific symptoms can alert the clinician to the possibility of a dissociative disorder causing the symptomatic presentation. The identification of MPD and ESD requires a thorough assessment and evaluation of the client over time, rather than rapid establishment of a firm diagnosis based upon the presence of signs and symptoms of a focal nature that satisfy the criteria for *DSM-III-R* categorization. Due to the fluctuating nature of their clinical presentations, dissociators often will have accumulated a diverse collection of diagnoses over years of involvement in the mental health system prior to the identification of their dissociative disorders. When the clinician suspects the possible presence of dissociative pathology and needs to make a rapid diagnosis, a "rule-out" of dissociative disorder should be added to the diagnosis of a focal dysfunction in order to document the continued consideration of this diagnosis.

CHARACTERISTIC PRESENTATIONS - CASES

To demonstrate the types of presentations actually encountered in practice, it is useful to consider characteristic cases.

These descriptions are composites, combining features that have been observed in a variety of clinical cases.

MPD. Sally is a 38-year-old white married woman who sought mental health services because of a recent exacerbation of chronic depression and anxiety. She had previously been involved in five episodes of outpatient psychotherapy with four different therapists, ranging in length from three visits to 10 months. Sally had been psychiatrically hospitalized on three occasions, for periods ranging from 2 weeks to 30 days (the limit of insurance coverage), once after self-mutilation behavior and twice in response to severe depression. None of these hospital stays had resulted in significant improvement, despite the use of many and varied medications and, on one occasion, electroconvulsive treatment. Hospital records indicated that Sally had posed no management problems, but that she had consistently remained aloof from other patients and staff, participating minimally in milieu activities and remaining detached in psychotherapeutic activities. She reported no lasting benefits from her outpatient psychotherapy, although she somewhat liked her third therapist, a supportive, patient woman who allowed Sally to manage the focus and pace of treatment. She felt that she had not been well understood by the variety of professionals with whom she had been involved, and reported negative reactions and deterioration in response to the wide variety of prescribed medications, including antipsychotics, lithium, antidepressants, and anxiolytics. Professional records revealed a range of psychiatric diagnoses, including major depression, bipolar disorder, generalized anxiety disorder, explosive disorder, and borderline personality.

Sally had superior intelligence, somewhat masked by her depression. She was vague and uncertain as an interview informant. She could recall nothing of her life prior to leaving home at the age of 18 and complained of frequent "blank spaces," periods lasting from several minutes to several hours for which she could not account. This information was disclosed in the fifth session when Sally reported, amid great distress, that at times she would find herself at various locations with no awareness of how she had gotten there. She was also upset about occasionally finding clothing and various objects (small toys, cosmetics, trinkets) in her possession which she had not purchased. Sally had never divulged these events to her prior therapists, due to her certainty that her fear of "being crazy" would be confirmed. Although

21

initially guarded in response to interview questions about hallucinations, Sally reluctantly acknowledged occasionally hearing voices inside her head (i.e., an adult voice at times telling her to hurt or kill herself and a childlike voice repeating "Daddy, don't hurt me . . ." at various times when Sally was in the proximity of male strangers). She described herself as "depressed as long as I can remember," stating her depression would sometimes become acutely incapacitating, with intense ego-dystonic suicidal impulses that frightened her. During the sixth session, when she had become more comfortable with her male therapist, Sally reported occasional aggressive behavior toward males, which she experienced as embarrassing, frightening, and extremely ego alien. In her mental status examination, no evidence of looseness of association or other signs of psychotic thought disorder were noted.

Sally initially claimed "a normal childhood in a normal family," although she was unable to recall significant events and was vague in her descriptions of people and events from her youth. At the time of her clinical evaluation, she reported no contact with her parents for 13 years, and maintained occasional contact with only one of her five siblings, a sister two years her junior. Once actively involved in outpatient psychotherapy, Sally gradually regained memory of an extremely traumatic history in a severely dysfunctional family, including incestuous sexual involvement with her abusive and intimidating father from the age of 6 to 15, incestuous involvement with an older brother from age 9 to 13, and frequently witnessing her father's physical abuse of her passive depressed mother. Sally recalled immersing herself in scholarship to escape these family experiences, receiving considerable affirmation and encouragement from teachers, and graduating from high school fifth in her class.

Sally complained of frequent severe headaches, which were unresponsive to analgesics. She also reported sporadic acute pelvic pain, although repeated gynecological examinations had failed to identify physical causes, while identifying the presence of vaginal scarring. Sally was being treated by a family physician for a chronic gastric ulcer and also experienced intestinal pain, frequent diarrhea, and constipation.

Comment. Although many other details and features could be added to this composite case description, this account has presented a typical combination of signs and symptoms characteristic of MPD. The diagnosis of MPD must remain presumptive until the clinician has had direct contact with an alter personality, whether during the first session or months into treatment. The combination of contemporaneous amnesia, ego-dystonic behavior and affect, and the history of repeated childhood trauma, leaves only that last criterion to be satisfied in order to resolve the diagnosis.

ESD. Susan is a 28-year-old white single woman who had initially sought services at a university counseling clinic due to increasing self-defeating behavior and declining academic performance. She was a graduate student in the humanities, and recently had found herself unable to concentrate. She had begun to miss deadlines and was receiving criticisms and warnings from professors regarding possible dismissal from the graduate program if her performance did not improve. Susan acknowledged a history of spotty academic performance, ranging from brilliant to severely deficient. She expressed acute anxiety about her inability to discipline herself and her growing sense of being out of control of her own behavior. She was drinking alcoholic beverages on a daily basis, which she found alarming. She also reported recent erratic automobile driving behaviors. With great shame, she reported that she had recently been engaging in casual sex with a variety of partners whom she met at a singles bar; this behavior was particularly disturbing to Susan, who was engaged to marry a young man with whom she had been involved for 2 years. She was quite convincing in her desperation and in her insistence that these behaviors were ego alien and reprehensible to her.

Susan described an extremely conflictual and unpredictable relationship with her mother, who had raised Susan alone after being abandoned by her husband when Susan was 2 years old. The mother, a deeply bitter and overwhelmed woman, alternated in her behavior toward Susan between episodes of physical abuse and angry rejection, and periods of guilty apology and overindulgence. She would frequently launch into enraged diatribes about the vileness of men, warning Susan to avoid loving or depending upon any man. Her abusiveness took the form of forcing weekly enemas on her daughter, slapping her face for no apparent reason, and refusing to speak to Susan for days. Her overindulgence was expressed largely in capitulation to Susan's demands, no matter how unreasonable. She was an isolated and lonely woman, who discouraged Susan's attempts to establish friendships with peers and participate in extracurricular and community activities.

23

Susan stated that she had long been aware of several "parts" of herself that responded quite differently to events: a depressed, ashamed "little girl part" which was interpersonally avoidant and tended to sleep and overeat for self-comforting, and a "hell-raising part," tending toward impulsive self-gratification, manipulative sexuality, and intense anger in the face of frustration. Susan described herself as serious, compliant, and overly responsible and voiced both fear of the impact on her own mood of the "little girl" and consternation about the behavior of the "hell-raiser." She denied awareness of events which led to intensification of the influences upon her behavior of these two ego states, which often would remain dormant for lengthy periods. Susan was aware of her increased emotional instability during the 2 weeks prior to beginning her menstrual period, particularly if she was under stress, but had no insight into any other patterns of ego-state activation.

Susan complained of constipation, sporadic bowel pain (her mother had used cold water in the enemas, causing abdominal cramping), and numbness in her extremities during times of intense anxiety. She was hypervigilant to physical sensations and their fluctuations, and presented hypochondriacal concern regarding feared illness (her mother's inconsistent nurturance had been predictably elicited by complaints of "not feeling well"). Susan reported significant fluctuations in her weight, with binge-eating periods followed by fasting and abuse of laxatives.

After exploring Susan's awareness of her ego-state structure and developing initial therapeutic rapport, the clinician easily induced hypnosis and established contact with the two ego states that she described. The "little girl," displaying depression and avoidance of eye contact, acknowledged that her growing sense of helplessness and futility appeared to sap Susan's energy and capacity for concentrated attention and effort. The "hell-raiser," presenting in a brash and seductive manner, stated that Susan was a "drudge" who didn't know how to have a good time, and bragged that she was going to continue to drink and seduce men for the pleasure of mastery over them. This ego state was steadfast in her commitment to destroy Susan's relationship with her fiancé before Susan became trapped by marriage and eventual parenthood. Subsequent hypnotic inquiry revealed a critical ego state, an "internalized mother," that frequently berated Susan whenever she received affirmation of positive relationship experiences; the affect and expression of this ego state exacerbated the depression and shame experienced by the "little girl."

Comment. This composite case description presents several characteristics of ESD, although these clients present many different symptom pictures, ego-state patterns, and degrees of dysfunction. The major cues signaling the presence of ESD are extremely dissonant motivations and affects, the presence of ego-dystonic impulses and behaviors, the sense of passive influence and lack of control over one's own behavior, the history of abusive and inconsistent early attachment relationships, the eventual hypnotic elicitation of ego-state presentations, and the absence of amnesia.

DIFFERENTIAL DIAGNOSIS

The differential diagnosis of MPD and ESD is difficult not only because a range of separately diagnosable signs and symptoms will typically be observed in dissociators, but also because of the symptom overlap with various diagnostic categories. In addition, no firm consensus has been achieved to date to guide the categorical diagnosis of the essentially dimensional phenomena of dissociation.

Coons (1984) has provided a thorough review of the differential diagnosis of MPD. Conservative in his approach, he requires the presence of amnesia for an MPD diagnosis, although, as previously noted, amnesia is itself a variable phenomenon within and between persons.

As suggested earlier, a wise strategy is to identify the role of dissociative process in the client's presentation, then gradually determine placement on the dissociative continuum as further information becomes available during treatment. Since ESD does not present the extreme dissociative features of MPD, it is likely that the majority of these cases will not be correctly identified. The phenomena characteristic of ESD can be accommodated by a clinical formulation that is not grounded in an appreciation of dissociation, but is focused instead upon traditional conflict views of neurosis or emerging views of borderline personality.

The vast majority of MPD cases come to the clinician carrying one or more misleading diagnoses, reinforcing the importance of the clinician conducting an independent diagnosis or confirmation of prior diagnoses rather than simply accepting and proceeding from the diagnostic efforts of others. MPD is frequently misdiagnosed as schizophrenia, based upon the client's acknowledgement of auditory or visual hallucinations. In fact, there is considerable overlap in *DSM-III-R* criteria for these two very different conditions, and many MPD clients will loosely satisfy the criteria for schizophrenia, paranoid type, which do not require the presence of looseness of association or other florid thought disorder. Beahrs (1982) has suggested that the absence of loose associations should eliminate schizophrenia as a possibility in the differential diagnosis of MPD. Another consideration is that MPD clients tend to locate their hallucinations within the head, while schizophrenics tend to locate their voices outside the body.

Bipolar disorder is another common misdiagnosis, based upon the observation of extreme swings of mood and energy in MPD. Bipolar swings, however, are typically slower and longer in duration than MPD mood changes, which are at times virtually instantaneous. At various times, MPD clients will tend to satisfy the criteria for major depression, atypical depression, dysthymia, or various anxiety/panic disorders. Ross and Anderson (1988) have identified overlap between obsessive-compulsive disorder and MPD in a small clinical sample.

Partial complex seizure disorder (temporal lobe epilepsy) may present with dissociative features, and there appears to be some degree of covariance between MPD and temporal lobe disorder. The fugue-like behavior of temporal lobe patients includes a perplexity not observed in MPD cases, and no alters will be discovered in temporal lobe patients. As Coons (1984) comments, the diagnosis of seizure disorder requires a sleep-deprived EEG with nasopharyngeal leads.

The diagnosis of alcoholism or chemical dependency often masks MPD or ESD. Particularly when alcoholic "blackouts" are reported, the clinician should remain vigilant for other dissociative features.

A general rule of thumb minimizes the risk of overlooking MPD: Whenever the client presents a history of extreme childhood trauma, many and varied psychiatric diagnoses, fluctuating symptoms, paradoxical or refractory response to psychiatric treatment, and baffling or atypical combinations of signs and symptoms, pursue exploration of dissociative phenomena. ESD should be considered whenever the client presents marked ego-dystonic impulse, affect, or behavior.

ALTER PERSONALITIES AND EGO STATES

Alters and ego states are complex phenomena, defying easy comprehension or description. Putnam (1989) defines alters as "highly discrete states of consciousness organized around a prevailing affect, sense of self (including body image), with a limited repertoire of behaviors and a set of state-dependent memories" (p. 103). Alters experience themselves as distinctly separate from each other and the host personality, sometimes unrelated and sometimes related as siblings. Some alters will carry this quasi-delusion to the point of imagining that they will survive victorious if they kill the host, with no recognition of "sharing the body" with other alters. Mention has previously been made of the distinct body images maintained by alters; these distorted perceptions resemble the types of distortions characteristic of hypnotic states, further supporting the consideration of MPD and dissociation as naturally occurring hypnotic phenomena (Bliss, 1986; E. Hilgard, 1977). Young (1988a) has argued that fantasy in childhood becomes elaborated, fixed by trauma, and dissociated into the specific structure of alters unique to each MPD client. This perspective is consistent with the strong correlation between reported childhood abuse, fantasy/imagery construction, and hypnotizability reported by J. R. Hilgard (1970).

Some alters are fully elaborated in function, while others are "fragments," holding an extremely limited range of memory, affect, and function. The degree of boundary differentiation and permeability separating alters' experience is also varied and ranges from denial of one another's existence to highly fluid, diffuse overlap of experience between states. Alters range in age from infancy to ages older than the client's chronological age and display developmental characteristics congruent with their subjective age. Both genders are commonly represented, with male alters in female clients usually serving as "bodyguards" against abuse or resulting from identification with a male abuser. In some MPD systems, animal alters will be found, as a result of the childhood fantasy creation of imaginary animal friends.

Alters/ego states are specialists in functions, and it appears that each alter/ego state expresses in concentrated form an affect, need, potentiality, or ego-defense function experienced over the client's lifetime. Although the initial dissociation and elaboration of alters occurs prior to puberty, once in place this defense becomes a dominant process throughout development. New

27

alters will often be dissociated in response to trauma or threat encountered in adulthood.

The conflict inherent in the co-existence of intensely disparate affects, self- and object-representations, and motivations within a person gives rise to the extreme distress and behavioral dysfunction observed in MPD. However, some systems are relatively cooperative, stable, and nonconflictual, allowing for freedom from psychiatric disturbance other than memory deficit and restricted affectivity. These high-functioning MPD cases may function at high levels of productivity and adaptiveness, showing no overt signs of dissociative disorder except during times of high stress.

Putnam et al. (1986) found a mean of 13.3 alters within MPD cases (median 9, mode 3), consistent with the findings of other researchers. Although no data are available, the number of discriminable ego states in ESD appears considerably smaller, reflecting less pervasive dissociation in response to less extreme or persistent trauma. Alters exist in complex structural relationships that can be graphically represented; often there will be a bipartite differentiation (e.g., "dark-side" alters vs. "light-side" alters) reflecting a division of "good" and "evil" motivations. There are commonly "layers" of dissociative structure, with some alters experiencing "lost time" and remaining amnesic to the existence and behavior of alters at "deeper" levels in the system.

Alters may present spontaneously during the early stages of assessment, either after a noticeable switch or by a smooth, outwardly undetectable transition of consciousness. The new alter may or may not announce his or her presence. It may take the astute clinician several sessions to identify an unannounced switch, which will typically involve a change in dominant affect, interpersonal behavior, and physical manner. The MPD client may present various "tests" to the clinician as a result of deep distrust of others and, often, a history of not feeling understood or helped by mental health professionals. A first test is sometimes to see if the clinician can spot the switch.

More often, no spontaneous switching will occur, and the first meeting of an alter will follow the clinician's building a strong index of suspicion of MPD, perhaps inducing hypnosis, and requesting the appearance of an alter (e.g., "I would like to speak with the part who cut Elaine's wrist last night"). The same approach is used in probing for the existence of ego states who, unlike alters, will not be able to present spontaneously, although they are able to influence behavior without full emergence.

It is not possible to present a comprehensive classification of all alter types or structures. Each dissociative system is unique, derived from the individual history of the client's experience. There are, however, certain types of alters that are commonly observed:

1. *Child.* The most frequent type of alter, the child may (a) hold the memory and affect of trauma, (b) serve as a positive resource by the development of particular competence (cuteness, social skill, intellectual prowess), (c) contain abuse-reactive aggression or depression, (d) contain hypersexuality in response to sexual exploitation, (e) serve as a protected and untraumatized child, or (f) serve as an unsuccessful bodyguard against abuse.
2. *Persecutor.* Coalescing in adolescence or adulthood in response to identification-with-the-aggressor, retroflection of rage, or rigid superego controls, this alter punishes the host and/or other alters with internal talk (auditory hallucination), bodily mutilation, or suicidal impulse. Persecutors were often earlier protectors.
3. *Avenger.* Displaying aggressive affect and behavior with the ultimate purpose of avenging early abuses, this alter may literally be homicidal.
4. *Protector.* Through threatening behavior, this alter seeks to prevent further abuses by others.
5. *Trauma Repository.* This type, regardless of age or other characteristics, serves to contain the memory and affect of trauma. This alter will recurrently re-experience the entire trauma as internally represented, as if it were contemporaneous.
6. *Host.* This alter is executive most of the time, serving as the system's "ambassador" to the external interpersonal world. To some degree, the host is typically amnesic for trauma and the existence of other alters, experiencing bewilderment and demoralization.
7. *Helper.* This alter provides general or specific adaptive functions (e.g., parenting skills, academic or vocational performance, mature judgment, social competence, etc.) or serves as a fantasy-based resource (e.g., a "good mother") not available in actual relationships.
8. *Narcissist.* This is a strong, energetic, and narcissistic alter displaying acting-out behavior, unconcerned about social norms or conformity demands, generally disdainful of the

ineffectual host, and often harassing and tormenting the host.

9. *Anesthetic Personality.* This alter feels no pain, is elicited by physical injury, and may in some cases engage in self-mutilative behavior.

10. *Center.* This alter, variously referred to as the Inner Self-Helper (ISH) (Allison, 1974), memory trace, or center alter/ego state, has an accurate and complete awareness of the client's history, an air of spirituality, an insightful understanding of the dynamics, distortions, and functioning of all alters, and a response to the therapist not contaminated by transference. Occurring in 50% to 80% of MPD clients (Putnam, 1989), this alter is an invaluable source of information and guidance for the therapist.

11. *Malevolent Alter.* Somewhat different from the persecutor alter (which usually can more easily become a positive resource to the client), this type is either (a) an introjection of the abuser, with toxic intentions, or (b) an alter identified with evil or the devil.

12. *Fragment.* This is an alter who is quite limited in function, less fully elaborated than other alters. A *special-purpose fragment* manifests a single skill or task performance (e.g., driving, cooking, parenting, etc.).

13. *Original/Birth Personality.* The psychological structure and developing identity from which the first dissociation occurs. Generally a child alter, and often not the host, this alter often does not present until late in treatment. Mixed opinions exist regarding whether or not the original must be the assimilator of abreacted trauma in order for the personality unification to take place.

This listing of common types and functions of alters does not do justice to the uniqueness of each dissociative system. There will often be several distinct alters of the same basic type, and not all types may be found in a particular client. A number of child alters usually will be formed and several different alters may hold different time periods or aspects of a single trauma. A wide range of developmental ages will be represented in the alter structure of the client, with corresponding effects upon the idiosyncratic features of the various alters. Relatively young alters tend to retain accurate memory for facts but have faulty and distorted attributions and meanings of events, while more mature alters generally will present more refined meanings and conclusions. A number of alters usually will be aware of traumas held by other alters, discussing these events dispassionately as if they happened to another person, which, in the subjectivity of dissociation, they did.

There will be only one true center in the client, yet in highly complex systems there may be "subcenters" which represent the center function for different subsystems of alters. Only one host will be observed at one time, but different alters may serve this function during different periods in the client's life. In some cases, the host is simply a superficial façade created by combinations of alters.

Some alters may be mute and somewhat autistic, particularly infantile alters or those who suffered extreme brutalization or forced drugging. A considerable range of ego strength and coping ability will be observed across alters within the MPD client, from stable and highly adapted alters to, occasionally, those who are psychotic. Misdiagnosis is often related to the separate presentations of diagnosable psychopathology by different alters. Various alters will display, in concentrated form, specific characteristics of emotionality and personality (e.g., rage, apprehension, distrust, gullibility, spirituality, contentment, shame, etc.) normally seen in more modulated and integrated forms in all persons. In addition, the dissociative compartmentalization and isolation of information across alters will be complex and, at times, variable. Some knowledge and experience will be shared among several or all alters, while more threatening material will tend to be more restricted in its internal representation. Putnam (1989) has provided a useful discussion of the phenomenology of alters and their machinations.

The effective clinician will avoid simplistic categorization of alters, in favor of thorough interviewing to determine the complex nature of each alter and the entire system. This process requires a careful and detailed cross-inventory of the information provided by different alters.

Some factors to be evaluated in the assessment of MPD include (a) the number of alters and complexity of the dissociative system, (b) the ego strength and functional resilience of the alters, (c) the extent and severity of nondissociative psychopathology, and (d) alter-specific risk factors (homicidal and suicidal motivation, psychoticism, substance abuse, self-mutilation, acting-out behavior) (Bloch, 1988). Kluft (1985b) has also identified several important dimensions to be assessed: (a) the resilience and power of the host to control other alters, (b) the degree of cooperation and conflict among alters, (c) the form of alters' interactions and influence on each other, (d) the importance of secrecy about traumas and the existence of alters, and (e) the degree of alters' investment in separate identity. As will be discussed later, this last factor is a most important determinant of treatment outcome.

ASSESSMENT

INTERVIEW

Timing and Rapport-Building. Proper timing of all clinical interventions is of the greatest importance at every step of the process of assessment and treatment of dissociative disorder. Moving too rapidly in either assessment or treatment will generate increased resistance and may overwhelm a fragile client with excessive affect and impulse, experienced by the client as retraumatization. The dissociative system has developed as a defense against trauma and has become the psychological structure of the client; once the correct identification of MPD is made and communicated to the client, the stability of this structure is disturbed and the client generally experiences an intensification of anxiety, impulse, and extreme affect.

The psychological trauma creating MPD, most often accompanied by failed early attachment relationships, leads to profound distrust of others. This deeply rooted distrust initially impedes the client's capacity to work honestly and effectively with a clinician attempting to perform the evaluation. The MPD system has facilitated the client's survival by remaining secret, and will tend to reveal itself only under conditions of trust and perceived safety. In addition, the client has usually encountered many experiences of being misunderstood by those who were expected to be helpers (parents, teachers, mental health professionals, etc.). These experiences simply add to the guardedness and unwillingness to disclose personal vulnerabilities. The astute clinician will be quite sensitive to the client's vulnerability and distrust, proceeding in a careful and patient manner throughout the evaluative process.

Before the MPD client will be able to reveal the critical information that the clinician seeks, he or she must experience some degree of rapport with the evaluator based upon trust and a sense of being understood by a person genuinely wanting to be of help. However, the client's dysfunctional history has probably led to a hypervigilance and hypersensitivity to the presence of deceit, disinterest, and domination. The clinician, therefore, must communicate genuine interest, empathy, and acceptance of the client's self-report and presentation in order for rapport to evolve. Although this rapport may develop rather easily with some clients, this preliminary step in the assessment process will take time with most clients and may be preceded by the client testing and carefully observing the clinician. The MPD client will generally need repeated reassurances, in words and behavior, of the safety of the clinical setting.

The clinician must avoid provocative behavior, or any conduct that might alarm the easily threatened client. If the client is uncomfortable with a clinician of the opposite sex, arrangements must be made for case transfer to a same-sex professional, and vice versa.

The clinician should respect the client's vagueness and inability or unwillingness to provide clear and coherent information in interviews. Frustration and impatience are readily sensed by these clients and interpreted as rejection. In the early stages of the relationship, this generally will lead the client to either resist exploration or abandon treatment altogether. The evaluator must be able to tolerate uncertainty, focusing primarily upon the development of the process of evaluation and treatment and giving up a need to elaborate content until the client is able to participate in that pursuit. It is essential to normalize the unusual, anomalous experiences that the client divulges, communicating the expectancy that all aspects of the client's problems will make sense as additional relevant information is revealed. At the same time, the clinician must avoid offering premature, facile interpretations and explanations, despite sympathizing with the client's bewilderment and often-desperate pleas for explanation.

Resistance is often intense, and deserves supportive respect as it is observed. Identifying, normalizing, and giving permission to the client to display and voice resistance will contribute to rapport-building and avoid rigidifying resistance past the point needed by the client in order to maintain equilibrium. The clinician should communicate appreciation of the threat experienced by the client in the clinical setting. Speculations about the nature of the client's difficulty should be offered tentatively, in a manner responsive to the client's level of readiness to gain more awareness of his or her dysfunction. However, the evaluator may well choose at times to prompt further exploration when the client appears stuck in resistance.

A major requirement for effective work with dissociative clients is a tolerance for a wide range of transference expressions and acting out. The intensity of dissociative transference rivals that of borderline clients and is often displayed in provocative and disruptive behavior. It is well to remember that regardless of the transference being expressed at the moment, there will be the varied transferences of different alters/ego states displayed at other times.

History. Gathering an accurate history in the evaluation of dissociative disorder is difficult and will continue throughout the assessment and treatment processes. The client will generally not be able to remember or communicate many aspects and details of his or her early life, and is likely to be confused about current experience as well; only over time will more pieces of the puzzle be revealed and begin to fit together. Each newly recalled event from the client's history will answer some questions and pose new ones, stimulating further inquiry and uncertainty. Clinicians unable to tolerate this uncertainty will find work with dissociative clients to be exceedingly frustrating.

Interviewing about the client's childhood experiences should be repeated many times throughout assessment and treatment. The client is likely to yield different information as the process unfolds, rapport is developed, repressive/dissociative barriers are weakened, and alters emerge. Often early interviewing will not elicit acknowledgement of the true extent and severity of family dysfunction that led to the development of the dissociative defenses. Challenging the client's response to interview is generally unwise and interferes with the establishment of rapport; it is better to note areas of suspected unreliability and unobtrusively resume interviewing in those areas later. The most effective style of interviewing is informal and supportive, avoiding an interrogative ambience that will heighten the client's anxiety and resistance. Questions regarding various aspects of history and experience should be intermingled in a casual conversational manner. The history can identify not only conditions that the client experienced and specific traumatic events, but also signs of ego-dystonic behavior that suggest likely dissociative process. Fluctuations in school performance and episodes of atypical behavior should be inquired about, and the client's capacity to attend to and explain anomalous events should be monitored closely. Inconsistent, contradictory, and vague accounts of personal history are characteristic of dissociative behavior, as is the client's complaint of faulty memory.

The clinician should inquire about instances of "lost time," periods of amnesia of several minutes' to several days' duration that are due to switches of executive control between the host and various alters. MPD clients will often have awareness of these episodes of missing awareness, and at times will have been informed by others of their unremembered behavior. The amnesic client is commonly reluctant to acknowledge these periods, so questioning must be careful, gentle, and persistent to gather this information. Amnesia for periods of childhood should be noted. Instances of depersonalization, derealization, "flashbacks" and other intrusive images, and hallucinations should be carefully probed and elaborated. The suspected dissociator should be asked whether he or she has ever been in possession of clothing, objects, drawings, or property with no memory of obtaining them.

The history must include information about the client's history of receiving mental health services, from childhood to present. The MPD client presenting in adulthood will often recount a litany of various treatments and diagnoses over years, none of which generated significant lasting improvement.

In a thorough discussion of diagnostic procedures, Putnam (1989) refers to the value of extended interviewing to elicit alters spontaneously. MPD clients are commonly able to suppress switching during brief interactions, but are likely to manifest alter changing as the evaluation session extends over several hours without an opportunity to escape observation.

Interviewing Significant Others. Those persons most directly involved with the client in daily life (spouse, siblings, lovers, friends, grown children) are potential sources of valuable data regarding the client and should be consulted whenever additional or corroborative information is sought and the client grants permission. Clinical contact with known or likely abusers of the client usually should be avoided.

These interviews should avoid leading the informants toward manufacturing magnified accounts of the client's dysfunctional behavior. A restrained and casual style of questioning ought to focus upon possible episodes of the client's uncharacteristic behavior and affect, or inconsistencies in the client's conduct that might suggest dissociative disorder. Material obtained from these contacts should be discussed with the client in order to minimize the breach of trust and also to monitor the client's response to these reports.

Hypnotic Inquiry. The observation of alter personalities is necessary to confirm the diagnosis of MPD, regardless of the presence of other indicators. Ideally, the first alter presentation will occur spontaneously and will allow the clinician to discriminate MPD from ESD. This spontaneous appearance is sacrificed when hypnosis is used prematurely. There will be times, however, when the evaluator appropriately decides to pursue hypnotic inquiry prior to spontaneous alter emergence. This approach is indicated particularly when rapid diagnosis is essential, when sufficient evidence to support an MPD diagnosis is available, or when obviously extant alters are avoidant of spontaneous emergence. The use of hypnosis is usually necessary to elicit ego states in confirming the diagnosis of ESD. It goes without saying that the clinician should be well trained and experienced in clinical hypnosis before attempting hypnotic work with dissociative clients.

Dissociators are typically hypnotic virtuosi, having employed trance repeatedly for years. Rapid induction techniques generally are sufficient, and these clients can be trained quickly to enter the hypnotic state in response to a verbal cue. Hypnosis allows easy switching between alters under the clinician's direction and control. Although hypnotic switching avoids the headache that many hosts suffer during spontaneous switching, the host will often initially resist hypnosis and hypnotic inquiry out of fear of loss of control or resistance to the diagnosis of MPD. This resistance must be managed gently and supportively, with reassurance that the host will remember as much as he or she wishes of the content of hypnotic work.

Once the diagnosis is confirmed, hypnosis is a most useful tool in the separate interview of various alters. This process aims to determine a number of factors in the evaluation, including (a) the ages, genders, and names of alters; (b) the developmental origins of the various alters; (c) the dominant affects and cognitive/perceptual styles of alters; (d) the survival functions (affect/impulse containment, trauma containment, protection, behavioral skill specialization, etc.) of the alters; and (e) the unique symptoms and dysfunctions of alters, which will in part determine the specifics of the treatment plan. It should not be expected that all alters will initially be revealed to the clinician; the elicitation of additional alters will continue throughout therapy, often almost until the successful end of treatment.

The usual procedure for the hypnotic elicitation of alters involves the development of at least light trance, followed by asking to speak to a particular alter, identified by name or behavior. It is wise to show great respect and consideration for alters by inviting their appearance and asking for ideomotor (finger-lift) signaling of their willingness to appear. The clinician must be prepared for the sudden appearance of alters presenting extreme affect and behavior, ranging from acute fear to intense rage and including all possibilities in between. Rapport must be developed with each alter separately, and each therapeutic relationship will be somewhat unique.

Alters will differ in their ability and willingness to serve as informants, and in their energy and duration of executive status. After conducting the appropriate interview, the clinician can simply request the alter to resubmerge, and then can either request another alter's appearance, give hypnotic suggestions appropriate to the entire system, or dehypnotize the host.

The clinician must simultaneously treat each alter as if he or she is a separate person, while maintaining an understanding that each alter is but a dissociated element of the client-as-a-whole. Failure to balance these two paradoxical perspectives will lead to repeated clinical errors.

TESTING

To date, there are no definitive psychological tests or interpretations of test data that will diagnose MPD or other dissociative disorders. The nature of dissociative phenomena makes it unlikely that such a measure can be developed; the switching of alters during testing creates artifacts in the test response pattern that would compromise the reliability of any test data. In addition, the host is generally oblivious to important dissociative signs and therefore is an unreliable informant in both testing and interview. Lovitt and Lefkof (1985) have found considerable difference between alters in their Rorschach performances, and various clinicians have identified inter-alter differences in Minnesota Multiphasic Personality Inventory (MMPI) profiles.

MPD clients generally produce MMPI elevations on scale F that often technically invalidate the protocol; other elevated scales include 2(D), 8(Sc), 4(Pd), 6(Pa), and 7(Pt). In general, MMPI profiles resemble those generated by borderlines. The clinician seeking more information on MPD and the MMPI should consult Bjornson, Reagor, and Kasten (1988), Bliss (1986), Coons and Sterne (1986), and Solomon (1983). Several critical items suggesting dissociative experience (items #156, 251) are often endorsed by MPD clients, but no profiles that discriminate between MPD and other disorders have been found.

Bjornson et al. (1988) have found MCMI (Millon Clinical Multiaxial Inventory) mean profiles for MPD clients characterized by marked elevation on scales 2 (Avoidant), 12 (Anxiety), 15 (Dysthymia), 8 (Passive-Aggressive), and 10 (Borderline). As with the MMPI, this pattern does not discriminate between MPD and other conditions, and thus cannot be used diagnostically except to support other findings.

E. E. Wagner, Allison, and C. F. Wagner (1983) proposed a set of Rorschach decision rules (Piotrowski scoring) to rule out MPD involving a high number of movement and color responses of a conflicting nature. However, several of the premises underlying their extremely conservative understanding of MPD are incongruent with current knowledge of the condition, and their theorizing about the expression of dissociation in projective responses is open to question. The permeability of dissociative barriers is a major variable across MPD cases, making it difficult to establish diagnostic rules that depend upon a single criterion of response type. Using the Exner scoring system with Rorschach protocols from three MPD clients, Lovitt and Lefkof (1985) identified a pattern of ambitensive status in all three subjects, indicating the absence of a firm, consistent style of coping with problems and demands, with vacillation and fluctuation between alternatives. Their results are inconsistent with those of E. E. Wagner et al. (1983), which is to some degree attributable to the different scoring systems used. At present, diagnosing MPD using the Rorschach is not possible; however, both of these approaches warrant further study.

There are two paper-and-pencil inventories of dissociative symptoms currently under development: the Perceptual Alteration Scale (Sanders, 1986) and the Dissociative Experiences Scale (Bernstein & Putnam, 1986). A third scale, the Questionnaire of Experiences of Dissociation (Riley, 1988), has recently been described. All three client-reported inventories of dissociative phenomena are promising, but all require further research and norming before clinicians will be able to rely upon them as diagnostic measures rather than as screening aids.

In summary, the clinician may find the use of standard psychological tests and specialized inventories to be helpful for screening or as sources of supportive information, but the problems that the dissociative process create in the routine testing situation make reliance upon formal testing to arrive at the diagnosis an unlikely prospect. The clinician must rely primarily upon interview-based assessment.

DIAGNOSTIC DIFFICULTIES AND RESISTANCE

Many of the difficulties that clinicians commonly encounter in the diagnosis and assessment of MPD and dissociative disorder have already been addressed. The fragmentation of experience caused by dissociation renders the client unable to develop and communicate a coherent chronology and perspective on the self. The result is a confusing clinical picture in which there are many and varied focal dysfunctions with no immediately apparent unifying pattern. Clinicians who seek to develop an integrated formulation of a case will find this process difficult, requiring great patience. More behaviorally oriented clinicians may be satisfied with a symptom focus, failing to ascertain the underlying dissociative structure of personality and experience. Only over an extended period of assessment will the dissociative nature of the client's situation be revealed and the pieces of the puzzle put together as information is gathered from a variety of alters/ego states.

One of the most prominent characteristics of the evaluation of dissociative clients is the steadily mounting complexity of the information with which the clinician must cope. As details of the client's past life and current internal workings gradually emerge, some of the uncertainty created by the client's vague and fragmentary account of experiences is resolved, but the psychological intricacy of the dissociative system is increasingly revealed. As alters emerge or are identified by other alters, the evaluator must sift through voluminous, often conflicting information in search of the dissociative structure and psychological themes that can help form a relatively coherent understanding of the client. The clinician's flexibility will be sorely tested as new information is divulged and evaluative formulations are repeatedly modified to accommodate the continuous influx of new data. Perhaps even more clearly than in the treatment of other types of disorder, the evaluative process with dissociative clients is never completed. Even as the clinician seeks to comprehend the complexity that the client presents, the system changes and shifts in response to the clinical work.

Other diagnostic difficulties are attributable to the symptom overlap between dissociative and other disorders and the problem of trying to fit the dimensional, continuous phenomena of dissociative process into categorical diagnoses. Identifying the presence of amnesia and significant ego-alien behavior, affect, or impulse, with a history of repeated childhood trauma, should alert the clinician to explore for other indicators of dissociative dysfunction. Further determination of the severity and pervasiveness of dissociation will allow discrimination between multiple personality disorder, ego-state disorder, and other forms of dissociative disorder.

Part of the problem of diagnosing these conditions is the client's resistance to correct identification. Typically, alters/ego states have formed and functioned in secrecy, which has served psychological and physical survival well. Discovery of their presence generally constitutes a massive threat to the client, both to the host alter, who typically seeks to maintain denial of the existence, affect, and experience of other alters/ego states, and to various other alters/ego states, who expect discovery to increase their vulnerability and danger. The host's denial of "the others" and the true nature of the disorder is common as the diagnosis is being developed and communicated, and will continue to wax and wane as treatment progresses, particularly during periods of increased stress. Some alters/ego states may desire the relief that accurate diagnosis and appropriate treatment offer, while others will obstruct the assessment process in an attempt to avoid detection. Alters will at times produce crises and other distractions in order to mislead the clinician as evaluation proceeds. Protective or malevolent alters may be hostile or menacing toward the evaluator, attempting to dissuade further exploration and discovery. All alters/ego states will, in direct or indirect ways, enact their own expectations of the clinician and of life. These expectations and derived behaviors will be quite varied and inconsistent, initially often tending to interfere with the establishment of a stable therapeutic environment.

The clinician whose frustration with this demanding and unsettling situation leads to rigid attempts to impose strict control on the assessment process will chase the client out of treatment or into further withdrawal and suppression, impeding the therapy. At the same time, one must not abdicate the responsibility to manage and structure the evaluation and treatment to prevent therapy from degenerating into chaotic acting out and continuous crisis. A middle ground must be found through experimentation and careful response to the productions of the client; the therapist needs explicitly to give the client considerable expressive freedom, along with the expectation of participating in the evaluation in a responsible manner. This position must be established at the outset of clinical contact to prevent treatment from becoming unmanageable and countertherapeutic. However, the clinician's intolerance of resistance will allow the sabotage of therapy by alters who act out the dynamics resulting from trauma and dissociation.

The severity and impact of resistance will be quite different from case to case, just as there will be a wide range of severity of dysfunction. Appearances are frequently misleading: Florid acting out and hostility will often dissolve into active participation in therapy if the clinician responds in a calm, nonreactive manner; however, a quiet, persistent refusal to relinquish dissociative defenses suggests a limited treatment outcome, regardless of the client's apparent cooperation with the therapist.

DISSOCIATIVE STRUCTURE

Once the diagnosis of MPD is made and shared with the client, determining the structure of the dissociative system is necessary before the clinician can work effectively with such a complex condition. Braun (1986b) and Putnam (1989) have described the commonly used process of mapping the system: The client and alters/ego states are asked to construct some form of visual representation (e.g., map, diagram, drawing, family tree, etc.) of the internal system, identifying the component parts by function, name, age, and other relevant information. These maps must be reviewed and revised regularly throughout treatment, because the earlier forms will usually omit some aspects of the structure in order to prevent threatening disclosures and protect hidden alters. Frequently, entire substructures will not even be known by many alters; whenever a particular alter acknowledges "lost time," there is another alter or layer of the system that was executive or internally active during that period. Alters and subsets of the structure that are deeply repressed once dissociated may lie quietly and undetected for years, but are likely to emerge as thorough and effective therapy proceeds.

Many dissociative clients will not be able to construct a map, but will gradually become able to provide some type of visual representation or cast of characters. Helper alters and center alters are generally the most reliable informants in mapping and other queries regarding the functioning of the system.

MALINGERING

The frequency of malingering and factitious MPD is likely to increase as information about the condition is more widely disseminated to the general public. Clinicians in forensic settings should remain skeptical of defendants who present dissociative phenomena when the avoidance of legal consequences for their behavior may be a motive. Kluft (1987b) has discussed the problem of simulation in forensic work, and suggests that *bona fide* MPD patients will tend to present features commonly thought by professionals to be indicators of malingering. There is no single, simple test that will discriminate true MPD from factitious MPD in an evaluation. The use of leading questions and sequential questioning regarding dissociation should be avoided in order to avoid suggesting MPD phenomena to the client. Kluft advises postponing treatment interventions and the use of hypnosis in forensic cases until an opinion about the presence or absence of MPD has been established because those activities are likely to cloud the evaluation process. The forensic setting continues to present major problems and complexities in the evaluation of dissociative disorder, as is found in the unresolved, equivocal judgments of opposing experts in the Hillside Strangler case (Allison, 1984; M. T. Orne, Dinges, & E. C. Orne, 1984; J. G. Watkins, 1984).

Some risk of factitious MPD in clinical treatment settings is possible when histrionic, attention-seeking clients are in close proximity to actual MPD clients, as in hospital settings, group therapy, or self-help groups. These false-MPD presentations generally will be dramatic, florid, and exhibitionistic in style and will often be characterized by a clear attempt to be diagnosed MPD that is quite atypical of most actual MPD clients. Despite not experiencing MPD, these simulators tend to be quite disturbed and may be revealed to present ESD.

RELATIONSHIP BETWEEN
ASSESSMENT AND TREATMENT

In light of the extended nature of the evaluation of dissociative disorder and the tendency of dissociators to conceal the nature of their condition until substantial rapport has been developed with the clinician, the distinction between assessment and treatment is more apparent than real. Most often, treatment based upon a nondissociative case formulation will be well underway before even an astute clinician will begin to suspect MPD or ESD. When such suspicion is experienced, the therapist should unobtrusively begin a reassessment of the client while avoiding disturbance of the therapeutic relationship.

Ideally, the clinician conducting the assessment will be able to continue working with the client in psychotherapy; under these conditions, there may be no discrete changes in the style of the clinical interaction. The sharing of the diagnosis with the client must precede establishing therapeutic goals and focus. When the diagnosis is shared, the client is likely to experience massive threat and destabilization, which must be managed carefully and supportively. The support of helpful alters should be solicited in the pursuit of restabilization and the prevention of risky regression or acting out.

Whenever the initial diagnosis has been made or suggested by a clinician other than the treater (e.g., an emergency psychiatric services worker, a credible colleague who is transferring the case for treatment, a forensic evaluator, etc.), the assessment of the specific features of the case must still precede the initiation of therapy. Prior to being able to be of therapeutic help to the MPD or ESD client, the clinician must obtain much information. Therefore, premature efforts to provide relief may create further problems for the client. The wise clinician will proceed slowly and gradually, preparing a solid base of information about the client and about the dissociative structure before attempting to institute change. The client is likely to experience some degree of fleeting relief in response to the therapist's support and effort to understand his or her distress; significant relief, however, depends upon the therapist's comprehension of the relationship between symptom and structure.

TREATMENT

GOALS

A variety of goals deserves consideration in the treatment of MPD and ESD, and the appropriateness of particular goals will be determined by a combination of factors. These include (a) the client's willingness and capacity to tolerate the rigors of intensive therapy aimed at relinquishing dissociative defenses, (b) the therapist's willingness and ability to provide such treatment, (c) the confounding effects of co-existent nondissociative psychopathology, (d) the degree of alter's narcissistic investment in continued independence of identity, (e) the presence or absence of adequate security and support in the client's current life situation to maintain the client through treatment, (f) the capacities of the client and therapist to establish and maintain an effective therapeutic alliance, and (g) adequate clinical resources (time, institutional support, treatment modality alternatives) to conduct appropriate treatment.

Many dissociative clients seek therapy in order to obtain relief from distress and dysfunction, but balk at the prospect of replacing dissociation, which has served them so well in surviving severe psychological and physical threat, with less distorting defenses that require assimilation and psychological metabolism of traumatic experiences. MPD clients often have suffered such a level and frequency of abuse and negation that dissociative defenses have been the only protection against psychosis or other debilitating psychiatric disorders. The clinician must respect the often intractable resistance that these survivors manifest regarding confrontation of their defenses.

When combined with other developmental factors that impede effective ego development, lifelong reliance upon dissociative processes to manage threat leads to considerable impairment of affect modulation and coping skills in severe MPD. These clients are incapable of withstanding the intense demands of an uncovering therapy without creating new alters or suffering iatrogenic deterioration. Often they are quite self-protective in their rejection of treatment approaches that are insensitive to their capacities. Even the strongest dissociative client requires consistent therapeutic attention to the development of effective ego skills before being able to benefit from confrontation of repressed and dissociated traumata; some clients are simply unable to manage such confrontation and resume their psychological development. In addressing a demoralization that he has observed among some professionals who previously were quite optimistic regarding the outcome of MPD treatment, Kluft (1989a) stated that the extreme level of dysfunction observed in many MPD clients now in treatment is greater than in his early successful cases from which that optimism arose (Kluft, 1982, 1986a, 1986b).

Kluft (1989a) also suggests that the therapist's unwillingness and lack of competence to manage the severe transference and countertransference disturbances that typify the treatment of MPD are responsible for clinician burnout. Treating MPD is arguably the most demanding, complex, and draining endeavor that a therapist can attempt. Many therapists are not willing or sufficiently well trained to perform this type of therapeutic work without paying an inordinately high price for doing so. Clinicians who are intolerant of the demands inherent in the treatment of borderline conditions should avoid the treatment of MPD; this will prevent unnecessary frustration of the therapist and further traumatization of the MPD client. The clinician must be able to tolerate poorly modulated affect, devaluation, extreme transference reactions by the client, strong countertransference feelings, intense acting-out behavior, vague and confusing information from the client, and severe discontinuities in the client's presentation. Some clinicians are comfortable with the supportive and restorative work of therapy, but are overwhelmed by the depth of the client's emotional pain encountered during abreaction of trauma. This limitation will interfere with the client's own ability to tolerate such work.

A major limiting factor in the treatment outcome is the severity and pervasiveness of the client's concomitant nondissociative psychopathology. Horevitz and Braun (1984) suggest that the more severe the borderline disturbance of the MPD, the poorer the prognosis. The therapeutic process repeatedly triggers regression and extreme behavioral reactions, and the severity of the host's and alters' character pathology and vulnerability to affective and cognitive decompensation in part determines the treatment goals that can be achieved. Clinicians who have treated MPD involving ritualistic abuse by satanic cults find that this trauma significantly complicates the treatment process by creating extremely severe psychopathology and polyfragmentation (Young, Sachs, & Braun, 1988).

The alters of adult MPD clients tend to develop some degree of narcissistic investment in maintaining separate identity and oppose therapeutic efforts to "fuse" personality functioning into a single self. Despite the therapist's preferences regarding fusion, it is the client system that will determine whether or not fusion is an acceptable goal. Alters tend to experience fusion or integration of personality as death, because they correctly anticipate the loss of identity and separate experience. The ideal outcome of treatment may be the merging of alters, each just a part or facet of the client's personality, into an integrated whole; however, the subjective reality of alters, seeing this process as leading to annihilation, often causes massive rejection of this option.

The MPD client's level of environmental support is a major determinant of treatment outcome. MPD clients are prone to involvement in dysfunctional and nonsupportive relationships in adulthood as a repetition of earlier patterns of experience. Faulty relationships often will produce retraumatization of the dissociative survivor of early trauma, or will at least create a stressful environment in which the maintenance of dissociative process is likely. Trauma survivors who continue to maintain originally traumatizing involvements (e.g., continued cult or incest participation, enmeshment with a dysfunctional family) obviously will not make significant progress in treatment. Other MPD clients have developed isolated, alienated lifestyles devoid of sufficient interpersonal support to allow management of the therapy experience. In order for the client to progress in therapy, there must be at least a moderate level of environmental stability and support; disturbances in the environment (e.g., loss of relationship or job, physical or emotional abuse, marital conflict, financial problems) will lead to therapeutic regression and deterioration. Kluft (1986b) has advised that therapy for dissociative child clients not be attempted unless environmental security and support can be assured. For adult MPD clients, the lack of adequate support will surely limit the possible outcome of treatment.

The capacities of both client and therapist to establish and maintain an effective therapeutic alliance is another factor in treatment. Although a variety of specific techniques and strategies are employed in the treatment of MPD and ESD, the therapeutic relationship remains the foundation and the most important ingredient of the therapy. The destructiveness and abandonment in primary attachment relationships experienced in childhood by most MPD and ESD clients results in significant impairments in ego development and interpersonal behavior. A proper therapeutic relationship provides an alternative to prior abusive or neglectful attachment relationships that is essential to restoring the client's self-esteem, self-confidence, capacity to establish successful relationships, and capacity to tolerate the demands of psychotherapy. In order to participate in the restorative relationship, the therapist must be able to tolerate the wide range and intensity of the client's transference and transferential acting out, must provide a flexible balance between support and confrontation, and must maintain stable boundaries in the interaction with the client. There will be many tests of the therapist and the relationship, and many of these tests will be quite subtle. Some therapists may not be able to negotiate the complexities of the therapeutic relationship with the dissociative client, and many severely disturbed clients will not be able to participate in a functional, effective therapeutic alliance. These failures often will lead to early termination of treatment and inevitably will severely limit the possible outcome of therapy.

Even when these factors are optimized, there remains the question of the adequacy of clinical resources necessary for effective treatment. Kluft (1987a) recommends a regimen of twice-weekly therapy sessions; the degree of departure from this schedule will determine the prolongation of treatment beyond the 2 to 5 years or longer duration of the typical treatment of MPD. ESD will often respond to much briefer and less intense therapy. Although there are no reliable estimates of the incidence of MPD and ESD, increased professional awareness and identification of childhood sexual abuse, incest, and physical abuse has improved the rate of detection of dissociative disorder, and it now appears that this type of dysfunction is much more common than was previously recognized. Clinical experience reveals that there are many more persons needing treatment of dissociative disorder than there are clinicians able to diagnose and treat them. Many MPD clients do not have the financial resources to seek private care and depend upon the services of public-sector agencies that often cannot devote sufficient professional time and attention to their needs. The range of treatment alternatives (e.g., art/expressive therapy, emergency hospitalization, medication, supportive group therapy) that are available and can be coordinated with the primary modality of individual psychotherapy will affect treatment outcome.

The treatment of the dissociative client can best be planned by deciding the extent to which support versus uncovering is indicated. When consideration of the prognostic factors discussed previously indicates limited potential for fusion or integration of personality functioning, the appropriate treatment will be primarily supportive, without confrontation of the dissociative defenses or uncovering of dissociated and repressed trauma experiences. This rehabilitative approach seeks to maintain and improve the client's functioning through monitoring, ego strengthening of the host and alters, and assisting the client's coping with *in vivo* problems and demands. As in the medical management of chronic disease, the emphasis in these cases is upon stabilization of the condition rather than upon cure. Work with the host and alters focuses upon improvement in internal cooperation, modulation of affect, control of impulse, and increased responsibility in daily behavior, with palliative relief of distress provided as needed. When the factors limiting prognosis involve the therapist's incapacity or insufficient clinical resources to provide more ambitious treatment, it is incumbent on the therapist to seek a transfer to another therapist or mode of treatment that may respond more fully to the client's needs.

To the degree that prognostic factors are more positive, the appropriate treatment will also include collaboration with the client in uncovering dissociated and repressed traumatic experience, restoring psychological metabolism of those traumas through managed abreaction, replacing dissociative processes with other defenses, and integrating personality functioning. Whenever in the course of this treatment the MPD client's coping capacities are overwhelmed, the therapist must retreat to supportive strategies until the client is again able to participate in the difficult work of confronting the dissociative process (Kluft, 1989b). Effective therapists will be quite flexible in titrating the proportion of support and confrontation in response to fluctuations in the client's capacities and functioning.

As in the treatment of borderline conditions, it is the therapist's responsibility to determine the direction of treatment in collaboration with the client, and to pursue that course consistently. Except as based upon fluctuations in the client's capacities, the vacillation between supportive and uncovering strategies will contribute to the client's increased confusion and resistance. However, many MPD clients will develop the capacity and willingness to pursue the more ambitious and restorative goals of the integrative approach if the therapist proceeds patiently in becoming acquainted with the dissociative system, helping the host and other alters engage in an effective therapeutic relationship, and addressing their behavior and affect control problems (supportive therapy). Perhaps the most simple statement of this approach to treatment was stated metaphorically by the late David Caul: "It seems to me that after treatment you want a functional unit, be it a corporation, a partnership, or a one-owner business" (cited in Kluft, 1987a, p. 370). Ego-state therapy similarly emphasizes the goal of improved client functioning over the elimination of separate identities in the treatment of MPD and ESD (Beahrs, 1982; J. G. Watkins, 1978; J. G. Watkins & H. H. Watkins, 1979).

In addition to the focus upon the dissociative process and structure, the effective treatment of these conditions requires attention to the shame, low self-esteem, and other sequelae of victimization. The clinician should become familiar with the growing literature regarding the treatment of survivors of sexual abuse (Bass & Davis, 1988; Briere, 1989) and incest (Courtois, 1988).

THE THERAPEUTIC STANCE

Effective treatment of dissociative disorder is grounded in the therapist's appreciation of the positive role of dissociation in the victimized client's psychological survival and equilibrium. Treatment requires a supportive, respectful therapeutic stance and a willingness to tolerate the client's severe, disabling distress and dysfunction. The therapist must avoid behaving in an authoritarian, critical, or controlling manner in order to prevent further traumatization or elicitation of pathological and countertherapeutic submissiveness. However, the therapist must also be willing to be authoritative in providing external structure and security at times when the dissociative client's internal structure fails. The therapist must be able to tolerate exposure to the client's intense emotional distress and primitive affects without overidentifying or withdrawing from the client, and must tolerate vague, metaphoric communication and a high level of uncertainty.

An appreciation of the unique subjective experience of the MPD client is essential for effective therapy and can be gained by reading *Many Voices* and *MPD Reaching Out* (newsletters by and for dissociative clients; see Appendix, pp. 85-86) and accounts of their experience written by MPD clients themselves (Chase, 1987) and by their therapists (Allison, 1980; LaCalle, 1987; Mayer, 1988). The effective treatment of dissociative disorder is focused upon the subjective experience of the client, which must be elaborated, validated as real, and gradually transformed into a tolerable form.

Stable self-esteem is essential for the therapist not to base his or her sense of professional competence upon the vicissitudes of the treatment and the MPD client's status. Mature, well-established ego boundaries allow the therapist to maintain a stance that is both helpful and self-protective. The client's demands for magical relief and exemption from the distress of experience must be tolerated and gently confronted. The therapist must consistently model for the client the possibility of reality-based survival, coping, and growth, as well as an acceptance of the pain of living and of the imperfectibility, irrationality, and unfairness of life.

In general, the therapist must provide sophisticated psychotherapeutic knowledge and skill, supplemented with a wide array of technical interventions designed to address specific problems. Discussions of particular techniques in the therapy will be found in the following resources: Beahrs (1982); Bliss (1986); Braun (1986a, 1986b); Caul (1984); Coons (1986); Greaves (1980); Kluft (1984a, 1984c, 1985c, 1986a, 1987a, 1988a, 1988c); Putnam (1989); Ross (1989); Ross and Gahan (1988); Sakheim, Hess, and Chivas (1988); and J. G. Watkins and H. H. Watkins (1988).

FORMS OF TREATMENT

The effective treatment of dissociative disorder must be eclectic and flexible; it must allow the focus to change as conditions require, while remaining clear regarding purpose and direction. The primary component is outpatient individual psychotherapy integrating a psychodynamic understanding of the client's condition with the supportive style of relationship previously described. The primary therapist must coordinate the client's participation in any other services or forms of treatment.

Due to their boundary deficits which make them particularly vulnerable to the behavior and distress of others, group therapy is difficult for dissociative clients. The presence of an MPD client in a therapy group of nondissociative clients will be disruptive and will interfere with therapeutic progress for all members. The dissociator's complexity and dysfunction will lead either to monopolization of the group's attention or to withdrawal and the masking of distress. Once the MPD client has achieved considerable functional stability and integration in treatment, homogeneous group therapy and support-group participation can be useful for the expansion of support and the development of interpersonal skills, if the therapist or facilitator is well versed in the treatment of dissociative disorder. ESD clients can often benefit from group approaches that focus upon interpersonal competence building, but the primary focus of treatment, inter-ego-state conflict resolution, can be addressed effectively only in individual psychotherapy. Grove (unpublished) is opposed to the group focus upon trauma experience for survivors of early trauma, due to the contagion of affect and contamination of trauma representations by the reports of others. Coons and Bradley (1985), Caul, Sachs, and Braun (1986), and Putnam (1989) have discussed the nature and problems of group treatment of MPD.

Marital and family therapy will not be effective in addressing the basic problems of the dissociative client, but can be useful adjuncts to individual therapy in dealing with specific relationship problems secondary to the dissociative disorder (Sachs, Frischolz, & Wood, 1988). Spouses, children, and others involved with MPD clients often benefit from collateral sessions with the therapist in which they gain information about dissociative disorder and strategic help regarding appropriate responses to the client. The children of MPD clients should be assessed for the presence of abuse, their own possible dissociative problems, and other psychopathology resulting from parental MPD (Braun, 1985; Coons, 1985). Spouses who are abusive or dysfunctional in their own adaptation should be offered services by other clinicians. Relatively functional spouses generally will need support in their efforts to cope with the stress and strain which is part of being married to MPD clients. Putnam (1989) presents a thorough discussion of marital and family approaches.

Art therapy and other expressive modalities are valuable components of the coordinated treatment of MPD. Artistic productions allow alters to communicate experience and affect in treatment in a manner often superior to purely verbal communication, and provide the clinician with information about the developmental levels of various alters (Fuhrman, 1988). Creative expression is also a powerful tool in the MPD client's abreactive work and other therapeutic work aimed at working through the effects of early traumatization. After years of secrecy and nondisclosure of trauma and distress, the self-expression of painting, drawing, sculpting, and writing are liberating for the client. MPD clients are often highly creative and may embrace these means of expression more quickly and comfortably than oral communication. Journal writing, letters/notes to the therapist, and poetry are favorite media for MPD clients and alters to give voice to their concerns, experiences, and identities. Puppet and doll play are particularly valuable forms of expression for child alters.

Other major forms of treatment are hypnosis, pharmacotherapy, and hospitalization. These therapeutic modalities will be discussed in more detail later in this monograph.

PRINCIPLES OF TREATMENT

Support and Management. Effective treatment of MPD and ESD requires a flexible balance of support and confrontation. The importance of genuine support has already been discussed, but support alone often will lead to prolonged and unproductive therapy that fails to catalyze the client's motivation to relinquish the reliance upon dissociation, resulting instead in the client seeking gratification by the therapist of unmet needs for affirmation and protection. Empathy for the extreme level of pain that the client experiences must be balanced by respectful confrontation of the unrealistic fantasies, distortions, and judgment errors of the host and alters. The client must be helped to attend to feelings, impulses, and memories that have long been obscured by the dissociative defense, and this process generates distress. Client and therapist alike should be prepared for the intensification of discomfort and symptoms that the client will experience when nondissociative processing of traumatic experience is begun.

Support ranges from providing encouragement, reassurance, and affirmation, to helping the client directly address specific problems of living and managing the client's situation when ego strength fails or crises overwhelm defensive protections. However, every act of support and management of the MPD client's experience must be carefully considered before implementation. Therapeutic interventions with MPD clients often result in unexpected negative results quite contrary to the desired outcome; therefore, such therapy requires even more anticipation of likely responses than in other types of psychotherapy. For instance, the therapeutic support given to the host or particular alters may be experienced as threatening by other alters, precipitating acting-out behavior. Therapeutic support may be misinterpreted as seductive by some alters, leading to responses that baffle the therapist who is unaware of such patterns of distorted perception.

In order to judge what degree of management is necessary to insure the client's safety, the therapist must maintain an accurate and up-to-date sense of the MPD client's and alters' fluctuating coping capacities. For example, the discrimination between severe suicidality requiring hospitalization and ventilation of intense affect that can be managed on an outpatient basis is not always easy. As with borderline clients, many MPD clients appear to become embroiled in almost continuous crisis, testing the patience and resourcefulness of the therapist. Toward the goal of helping the client develop increased coping skills, the therapist should avoid taking responsibility for managing aspects of the client's conduct and decision making that the client is capable of managing. Various alters may test their expectations of abandonment and indifference from others by creating demands for the therapist's time and caretaking that appear to be contrived or exaggerated. These events should be explored thoroughly with various alters before responding.

Relationships with Alters and Ego States. One of the unique aspects of therapeutic work with dissociative disorders is the engagement in multiple relationships and transference-countertransference problems with a single client. The therapist's resonance to these various relationships, needs, demands, and distortions is an important ingredient of effective treatment because all significant alters/ego states must eventually participate in the psychotherapy if it is to be successful (Watkins, 1978). Such participation will occur only in an inviting environment in which each feels accepted, affirmed, and safe. When confronting or controlling the behavior of a particular alter/ego state, a punitive, judgmental attitude must be avoided and the original function of that alter/ego state must be explicitly acknowledged and affirmed even as limits are placed upon problematic behavior.

An ability to relate effectively with alters/ego states of widely varied levels of development is essential. Child alters will tend to perceive the therapist as an abuser, parent, or friend, and the therapist must be able to accept the developmental limitations encountered in the child's construction of the meanings of experience. Adolescent alters/ego states generally will present the narcissism and rebelliousness seen in nondissociative adolescent clients and will require firm limits in the context of an affirming relationship. Acting-out alters/ego states must be constrained. Depressed and apprehensive alters will require support and reassurance. Trauma-repository alters must be given strong support even as they are asked to continue to hold trauma memory and affect until the host and the dissociative system are sufficiently strengthened to assimilate that material. All alters should be directed toward increased verbal and creative expression of their affect and problems instead of engaging in impulsive, destructive, and self-defeating acting out. Affirmation of the affect and experience held by alters will work to counter the disaffirmations that resulted from abuse and the attempts to deny the abuse. The expressive opportunities for alters in therapy can be extended if the therapist invites alters to mail in notes, poems, and drawings between sessions; these productions should be acknowledged and discussed at the next session.

Each component of the dissociative system will present a somewhat unique style of thinking, associating, and constructing meaning, often built around the "fixed ideas" identified by Janet (van der Hart & Friedman, 1989) in his study of hysteria and dissociation. These fixed ideas are images, thoughts, or associations related to traumatic or threatening experiences that retain intense emotional charge because they are isolated from neutralizing, metabolizing, and integrating ego processes. The therapy process must identify and modify these distorted and rigid artifacts of earlier experience, but this will not occur through rational discussion and correction. The therapist who attempts to convince the dissociative client of the error of these ideas will be no more successful than the clinician who attempts to dissuade the paranoid client from his or her delusions. Confrontations of misattributions, cognitive/perceptual distortions, or self-defeating patterns of behavior must be accompanied by validation of the client's feelings as real.

In relating with alters/ego states, the therapist should avoid "playing favorites," supporting some and ignoring others. Different alters will require attention and therapeutic focus at different times throughout treatment, but once an alter has presented to the therapist, regular inquiry about that alter's status is important. The therapist must relate effectively, supportively, and helpfully with alters, seeking to improve the contribution of each alter to the client's overall functioning. However, excessive gratification of alters' needs for acknowledgement and affirmation may create an iatrogenic impediment to integration of the dissociative system. The therapist must remember that each alter/ego state is but one facet of the client's true personality. The overall goal of treatment is to strengthen the functioning of the entire personality system, not to strengthen the dissociation of alters via mirroring and promotion of alter individuation. The therapy time devoted to the development of greater ego strength and identity in the host and in the "original" personality should exceed the amount of time spent in strengthening the separate alters. At the same time, alters who become more effective in contributing to organismic functioning will provide greater resource and support of this overall improvement.

Persecutor alters, malevolent alters, and toxic-introject alters present particular problems in therapy. Putnam et al. (1986)

found that 53% of a large clinical sample of MPD patients reported "internal homicide" behavior (attempts by one or more alters to kill the host or other alters), with 34% presenting self-mutilation, often as punishment of one alter by another. Persecutor alters are either previously helpful alters who have become impatient or angry alters who redirect and act out their rage onto the host or other alters. They generally will respond to firm, patient therapeutic efforts to redirect and channel their hostile impulses in more appropriate ways, learning to identify the appropriate targets of anger and to ventilate rage without acting out. In the meantime, it is essential to monitor self-destructive risk firmly to limit dangerous persecutory behavior.

These persecutory, malevolent, and toxic introject alters typically display child or adolescent development. Malevolent alters have identified with evil motivations of others or serve as the crystallization of the client's aggressive, destructive impulse. Toxic-introjects are internalizations of attachment figures who have previously brutalized or abused the client. These alters are more difficult to redirect and often require containment until the dissociative system becomes sufficiently strong and self-promoting to counter and reject these self-destructive motivations. Toxic alters often will respond to judicious confrontation of the identity confusion that leads them to consider themselves as part of the abuser rather than as part of the client. Defining the essentially protective function of their identification with the abuser will cause confusion initially, but eventually will enable the establishment of more effective and protective behaviors.

The most therapeutic approach to persecutory and acting-out alters/ego states is to address their origins, experience, and function, guiding them into more positive expressions of affect and impulse. When this strategy is insufficient, contracting for behavior control or enjoining other alters to manage this problem behavior is the next step. Hypnotic suppression of an alter for a period of time can be employed when strong and immediate risks to safety and effective coping are observed. Putnam (1989) and J. G. Watkins and H. H. Watkins (1988) provide illuminating discussions of their work with persecutor and malevolent alters. Since these problematic alters are dissociated aspects of the client's personality, there should be no thought or discussion of eliminating any alter, no matter how troublesome.

The Inner Self-Helper (ISH). The inner self-helper or "center" is a fascinating and important phenomenon in MPD. This alter is aware of all alters, has existed from the beginning of the client's life, and possesses judgment and perception uncontaminated by the ego-destructive events that led to dissociation. There may be several "subcenters" who serve the same function for different substructures of alters. It is not yet clear whether or not all MPD clients possess an ISH, but when an ISH is present, it can be an invaluable asset to the treatment, serving as a consultant to the therapist and providing information about the system's complexities and internal reactions to both life events and the therapist's behavior. ISHs also can provide guidance regarding therapy choices and direction, warning the therapist of imminent problems and crises. Putnam (1989) advises respectful attention to the suggestions of ISHs, but cautions against indiscriminant adherence to those suggestions and abdication of therapy direction to the ISH. Comstock (1985) sees the ISH as a somewhat spiritual, transcendent component of personality and offers a number of intriguing ideas about working with the ISH in therapy.

A sound procedure is to ask early in therapy to speak with "the part who knows everything and everybody, the Center." When using this procedure, the therapist must accept that an ISH will decide when to present to the therapist and when to participate in the treatment. The ISH will not necessarily tell "the whole truth" in response to the therapist's questions, having a greater allegiance to the system and its protection than to the therapist. ISH utterances can frequently be identified by their enigmatic, oracular style, which often requires careful deciphering. The therapist can request assistance in resolving specific questions and can ask the ISH for between-session notes or spontaneously provided information, as the ISH sees fit. In some cases, the ISH will be unable to become executive and instead will arrange to communicate with the therapist through a mediating alter. The ISH generally lacks in physical power and direct system influence what it possesses in information and wisdom.

Since the therapist can have direct awareness only of an extremely limited part of the dissociative client's experience, behavior, and internal machinations, there inevitably will occur many confusions, misunderstandings, uncertainties, and miscommunications in the therapy. The ISH, as well as other helpful alters, can be valuable in the treatment when the therapist's humility allows acceptance of correction and direction from within the client.

Development of a Sense of Self. The client presenting dissociative disorder most typically will also manifest disturbances in his or her sense of self, secondary to the pervasive attachment failures and splitting accompanying abuse. Treatment of this aspect of the client's dysfunction will rely upon the support and acceptance available in the therapeutic relationship and will focus upon the client's gradual development of ample, integrated self-representation and stronger ego boundaries between the self and others. Supporting the client's grieving over the absence of adequate attachment experience during the formative years, the therapist must accept that this developmental deficit is likely to have resulted in irreversible effects upon the client's vulnerability to depression (Bowlby, 1980).

Development of Enhanced Coping Skills. The early reliance upon dissociative defenses generally renders the dissociative client deficient in the normal development of effective and mature skills for coping with stress and the demands of daily living. In order for the client to function better and to become capable of metabolizing dissociated and repressed traumatic affect, therapy must emphasize the development of enhanced coping skills. This remedial work requires an active teaching style of treatment in which the therapist explicitly identifies the coping impairments exhibited by the host and alters and provides direct instruction and modeling of more accurate perceptions and perspective, more effective management of affect and containment of impulse, and expanded alternative responses to situations. Strong affirmation and reassurance must be provided as needed. In part, the balance between therapeutic support and an expectation of the client's autonomous management of problems determines the degree of regressive dependency manifested by the client, who often will seek to avoid confronting the difficulties of life.

A wide range of techniques and strategies is available in this work, limited primarily by the creativity of the therapist. Different alters/ego states will present different needs and coping deficits, and will require different interventions. The enhancement of ego strength and coping competence among the host and other alters will precede the development of those skills in the system as a whole. Training in stress management, affect and impulse control, behavior control, and problem solving is helpful to impulsive and affect-holding alters. Inhibited, withdrawn alters will benefit from a focus upon increased expression and self-assertion; shame-based alters will require supportive resolution of their shame in order to become more functional (Bradshaw, 1988; Kaufman, 1985). Overwhelmed or depleted alters require therapeutic help in escaping from distress or subjective threat. In order to be effective, these interventions must be offered in a manner and form appropriate to the developmental level of the alter toward whom they are aimed.

Integration of Experience. As ego strength and coping skills develop, an additional focus of treatment is the client's reowning of the experience, affect, and dissociated aspects of the personality. Dialogue between alters/ego states should be encouraged, in the pursuit of coordination and integration of the system's dissociated skills, resources, knowledge, affect, and experience. The therapist can mediate this process, interpreting and advocating the interests and perspectives of alters to each other. A useful technique toward this end is "internal group therapy" (Caul, 1984), in which the host and other alters meet and confer, either addressing specific problems and decisions requiring collaborative attention, or simply becoming acquainted and sharing views and feelings. The therapist should repeatedly emphasize the value of partnership among alters/ego states, characterized by adherence to "the golden rule," negotiation of compromise solutions to conflicts, and appreciation of the legitimacy of different perspectives and motivations.

Alters should be urged to write notes to the host regarding their feelings and preferences about everyday situations and therapeutic material or to use a tape recorder to talk with the host if the host does not hear or respond to the internal dialogue. Caul (1984) discusses the usefulness of videotaping therapy sessions because it allows the host to observe alters in action. However, videotaping should be postponed until the host has initially accepted the diagnosis and expresses a readiness for watching the videotape.

As treatment proceeds and alters gain acceptance and awareness of each other, they should be encouraged to "time share," a process of simultaneous sharing of executive control of behavior among two or more alters who each can contribute positively to managing a situation while retaining their separate identities. The therapist should urge alters of similar functions (e.g., protectors, helpers) to become internal allies in order to optimize their effectiveness. Strong alters can serve as a team to support weaker, distressed alters. Nurturant alters should be encouraged to nurture hurt-child alters. This strategy is analogous to family therapy interventions designed to catalyze change in the structure of relationships between family members.

The emphasis upon the development of increased dialogue, support, and cooperation among alters should precede therapeutic work on abreaction and the integration of traumatic experience. Further development of enhanced ego strength and competence will result from this integrative focus, and the crises resulting from inter-alter conflict and warfare will subside as alters become less internally contentious.

Modulation of Affect. Related to the therapeutic development of increased ego strength and integration of experience, the development of affective modulation is an important focus of treatment. Alters presenting intense affect (rage, shame, fear, anxiety/panic, depression) and impulse (hypersexual, self-mutilative, suicidal, homicidal, aggressive, submissive, self-defeating) generally will derive benefit from repeated opportunities to ventilate affect in therapeutically guided and supported ways. Some alters may respond well to hypnotic techniques (to be discussed later) aimed at affect containment and controlling the intensity of feelings. Encouragement to draw, paint, and write will allow alters to develop new modalities of expression and catharsis. The "silent abreaction" technique (H. H. Watkins, 1980) allows alters to discharge intense affect (particularly anger) internally, without the disruptive effects of loud verbal ventilation in the office setting.

Attempts to modify affective representations by rational confrontation or reframing generally will be ineffective, and often will be experienced by alters as devaluation and rejection. It is essential to validate experience and resultant affect, and gradually to nudge the host and entire dissociative system toward assimilating and metabolizing previously dissociated experience and affect. Analogous to the metabolic processing of food nutrients, this emotional metabolism allows the breakdown of expressed affect into its meanings and informational value. This process helps the client learn new understandings of early experience and helps resolve fixated feelings. For example, expressing anger about childhood exploitation and receiving support and affirmation from the therapist will facilitate the client's emotional completion of that early experience (E. Polster & M. Polster, 1973), thereby resuming full involvement in here-and-now experiencing.

Abreaction and Catharsis. Abreaction is the process of reliving an intensely affect-laden experience, the memory and affect of which has been repressed and dissociated. In MPD and ESD, abreaction is an essential component of thorough treatment and is aimed at resolving dissociation and restoring the integration of personality. Usually the host alter, one or more "anesthetic" alters, or the "original"/"birth" personality experiences the revivification and engages in the subsequent debriefing and relearning processes. From a systems-focused perspective, successful abreaction requires a wide-ranging reliving and relearning throughout the dissociative system.

Whereas traditional psychodynamic therapy has thought of abreaction as the process necessary for any client to release previously repressed affect and memory related to trauma, the presence of dissociation requires a distinction between abreaction and catharsis. Abreaction refers to revivification that crosses dissociative barriers, while catharsis refers to the revivification process that is confined to a single alter/ego state and does not result in cross-barrier integration of memory and affect. Cathartic ventilation by an alter will lead to some degree of palliative relief from the release of affect, but abreaction is necessary for the relinquishing of dissociation to occur.

Considerable resistance will generally be encountered when abreaction is imminent. Not only is the abreactive experience extremely painful, but also repressing alters will seek to avoid the disclosure of "secrets" and shame-inducing events. At times, alters will resist abreaction when their "reason-for-being" has been to hold traumatic experience and to protect the repressing alters from such threat; they will oppose abreaction out of fear that they will be unneeded when abreaction is complete. The entire process of abreaction and metabolism is contrary to the function of dissociation, and this constitutes a threat to the dissociative system. Various alters, including the host, often will fear that the experience of intense trauma-related affect and knowledge will overwhelm their coping capacity.

MPD clients frequently will present prodromal signs of an imminent abreaction. These may include acute depression as an attempt to suppress all affect and energy or fragmentary hallucinatory images of the episode to be revivified. Spontaneous abreaction, particularly early in treatment, often is triggered by anniversaries of trauma, other significant events, or situational stressors. These spontaneous abreactions may precipitate crises exceeding the capacities of the system to remain stable and some-

60

times lead to the creation of new alters. Simply re-experiencing trauma without structured re-examination of the experience will not result in therapeutic progress, and will retraumatize the client. Once the client displays enhanced ego strength, planned abreaction allows more control and pacing of the revivification of intensely emotional experience.

The essential retrieval and assimilation work of abreaction occurs within the client, and will be impeded by distracting dialogue with the therapist. The major work for the therapist during abreaction is (a) to monitor the client's status and physical safety, (b) to keep the client grounded in reality via reflection of what the client is expressing and occasional reminders of the present time and treatment context, and (c) to keep the client involved in the abreactive experience until its natural conclusion. The therapeutic input from the therapist comes during debriefing and exploration of the meaning of the experience to the client. The debriefing process helps the adult client develop a more mature comprehension of his or her life that can be metabolized more easily than the childhood representations previously encapsulated by the dissociative process.

Successful abreaction requires the full experience of affect, not just the factual knowledge of the traumatic event, and the therapist can support the client's affective experience by providing guidance in managing the abreaction. The client can be hypnotically seated in a chair that has controls (knobs, switches) for controlling the speed and intensity of the revivification. Another possibility is to urge strong and supportive alters to "blend" with the host or other abreacting alters for reassurance, support, and greater ego strength. A variety of other interventions will help the client withstand the rigors of this emotionally powerful experience, but none should interfere with the actual retrieval of the repressed and dissociated experience.

At the conclusion of an abreaction, the client is likely to be briefly disoriented and fatigued. For this reason, abreactions should begin early in sessions in order to allow sufficient time for full revivification, reorientation, and debriefing before the client must leave the office. Considerable confusion, experiential restructuring, and reactive emotional response may occur for hours or days after the client leaves an abreactive session. Therefore, access to the therapist by telephone can be an important form of support during periods of abreactive work.

It is generally agreed that abreaction of all significant traumas is essential to full reintegration of experience and personality.

This can make abreactive treatment appear interminable for clients who have suffered frequent brutalization or other traumatization. Young et al. (1988) reports that MPD clients exposed to ritualistic abuse by satanic cults or other abusers are known to present particular problems during abreaction due to the severity of their traumatization, their frequent participation in the abuse or brutalization of others, and the likelihood of strong counter-therapeutic programming.

After initial successful negotiation of several abreactions, some clients may be able to manage abreactive episodes at home without the therapist's presence for support. These abreactions will require careful monitoring and thorough debriefing in therapy sessions. Some clients may re-repress traumatic experience after abreaction, which generally indicates insufficient ego strength to hold the experience or insufficient debriefing to allow transformation and metabolism of the trauma. Some traumatic experiences may require several revivifications before they can be metabolized, and some extremely severe trauma may not be assimilable without damage to the client's self-esteem and coping skills.

Premature initiation of an abreaction treatment focus by the therapist will be counterproductive and traumatizing to the client. If abreactive work is to be successful and progressive, it must be preceded by the development of a strong therapeutic alliance, the exploration of the dissociative structure, the development of internal dialogue and cooperation, and the enhancement of ego strength.

For more information regarding the abreactive process in therapy the reader should consult Comstock (1986, 1988), Putnam (1989), Ross (1989), and H. H. Watkins (1980).

Respecting Resistance and Capacity. The client's intense resistance to therapy will take many creative forms over the course of treatment, and the effective therapist will show genuine respect for such resistance as basically a reasonably successful self-protective repertoire of behavior developed by the client in response to a history of overwhelming traumatic experience. Different alters/ego states will manifest different styles of resistance ranging from numbing and restriction of affect to extreme acting out. As discussed earlier regarding resistance to the initial assessment phase of working with dissociative disorder, the therapist must tolerate these efforts to maintain the homeostatic balance of the system, interpreting and explicating various resistance maneuvers and helping the client work through them rather than acting out. Recurrent reassurances of the safety of treatment and of change should be offered, along with support of the apprehension experienced by alters/ego states. There must be a compromise between the therapy pace preferred by the therapist and the rate of treatment tolerable to the client, with sensitive response to the exacerbations of distress or behavioral symptoms that signal an excessive level of threat.

Chu (1988) has defined several areas of resistance in the treatment of MPD: (a) resistance to the exploration of repressed trauma, (b) resistance to trust in the therapist and engagement in treatment, (c) resistance to relinquishing dissociation and repression, and (d) resistance to integration. Each of these foci of resistance signal serious perceived threat to the integrity and survival of the dissociative system, thus creating intense, often desperate, behavioral expressions. Most therapists of MPD can recount examples of clients' acute acting out or ventilation of resistance in response to the therapist's inadvertent disregard of resistance signals. Resistance is not some obstacle to therapeutic victory, to be blasted through by confrontation and directive therapy. Instead, resistance should be viewed as an important expression of the client's fear. Remember, dysfunctional defenses cannot be relaxed or relinquished until relative security is experienced and newer, more effective means of self-support and self-protection have been developed.

Resistance is a major factor in all psychotherapy (Strean, 1985; Wachtel, 1982) and is a major focus of interpretation and change in psychodynamic treatment, which is structured around the interpretation of transference, defenses, and resistance. In a thoughtful discussion of resistance in MPD treatment, Putnam (1989) argues against the therapeutic focus on resistance, except when it interferes with the central work of therapy. This approach avoids the risk of allowing the client's resistance to dominate the treatment and divert effort and attention from therapeutic progress.

A basic resistance in MPD that does require repeated confrontation is the client's resistance to the acceptance of reality. Dissociation is initially a way to avoid the acceptance and assimilation of extremely harsh and destructive realities in childhood, and subsequently leads to ongoing distortion and rejection of other realities. The client must be moved gently toward greater acceptance of the brutal realities of the past as well as current realities and needs considerable support in grieving losses while coming to a more accurate understanding of events, affects, and their meaning.

Respect of the client's resistance must be accompanied by respect for the client's capacity to tolerate threat and traumatic revivification. The therapist's thorough comprehension of ego strength and its manifestations will allow sensitive monitoring of the client's functioning and tolerance of the threat and distress resulting from therapy. Regression, frequent switching, cognitive/affective decompensation, and severe demoralization are among the indicators that the client's capacity to assimilate threatening information is being overwhelmed. It is the therapist's responsibility to remain aware of the fluctuating ego strength of the client, managing and pacing the processes of abreaction and reowning of repressed and dissociated material.

System Balance. The complex psychological structure of the dissociative client has evolved to manage intense needs and affects, severe loss, extreme trauma, and other threats to psychological survival. This dissociative system of alters/ego states and the relationships among them has developed a balance, however tenuous. The therapeutic process disturbs that balance and to varying degrees destabilizes the system. The therapist must constantly monitor the status of the system's stability, working to contain the effects of destructive, masochistic, and self-defeating motivations, providing support to highly strained alters/ego states, and strengthening those alters/ego states seeking more effective, reality-based, and mature approaches to the demands of life.

A major principle of ecology that applies to all system-impacting interventions states: "You can never do just one thing." All actions create complex rippling effects and reactions, which should lead to caution by the therapist in planning interventions in the treatment of dissociative disorder. Anticipation of likely responses to possible interventions can allow the therapist to be prepared for the disruptions of the dissociative system that accompany the changes wrought by therapy. The nature of system balance and the imbalancing effects of the therapy should be fully discussed with the client in order to reduce bewilderment and alarm.

Transference and Countertransference. The transference and countertransference phenomena encountered in the treatment of dissociative disorder are intense. The unmodulated affect and motivation of the dissociative client often will lead to powerful transferential acting out similar to that of borderline clients, and the demands of the therapy elicit strong reactions within the therapist. Transference reactions create ongoing disturbances of treatment, testing the perseverance of both client and therapist.

Each alter/ego state will experience the therapy and the therapist differently, expressing the highly charged emotions that result from extreme perceptual distortion. These transference events require careful identification and exploration in a relationship context of acceptance, constancy, and containment of countertransference; this is possible only when the therapist maintains strong, mature ego boundaries. The dissociative client has developed complex intrapsychic boundaries between alters/ego states to compensate, in part, for poorly developed boundaries between self and other. This interpersonal boundary deficit will be corrected only when the therapist can tolerate its effects and patiently lead the client toward more stable and reality-based interpersonal relations.

Five common types of negative transference in dissociative disorder are found in various proportions in particular alters/ego states: erotic/seductive, hostile/aggressive, dependent/clinging, withdrawn, and masochistic. The flavor of an alter/ego state's transference reveals much about the developmental origin, expectancy, experiential history, and function of that component of personality. Transferential acting out is both a natural result of the projection of these strong affects and a form of testing the therapist, seeking to confirm interpersonal expectancies (self-fulfilling prophecy) and establish the nature of the therapeutic relationship. Since some alters/ego states have had little experience with positive attachment relationships, they will attempt to define the therapeutic relationship as consistent with their dysfunctional experience. The therapist must identify and interpret these behaviors, guiding alters/ego states away from acting out and toward reflective verbal expression of transference, gradually leading the client in the direction of more accurate, discriminating interpersonal perception and self-perception. Child and adolescent alters/ego states and those holding severe trauma and distress will have particular difficulty with this part of the work. The therapist will need great patience; he or she must exercise great care to avoid confirming the client's expectancies and recapitulating prior relationships. Considerable dependency and ambivalence must be tolerated in these treatment relationships, with discrimination between reparative and regressive elements of dependency.

Shame-based alters/ego states require careful support and affirmation before the crippling effects of their shame can yield to healthy, realistic self-esteem. Aggressive, angry alters/ego states typically conceal great hurt, fear, and vulnerability, which must be identified and addressed before the aggressivity will subside. Erotic, seductive alters/ego states often act out their systemic role toward the therapist; in addition to enactment of a previously learned pattern of relationship behavior, this acting out is frequently an attempt to establish control over the therapist. Often control over abuse (and an abuser) via sexualized and seductive behavior provided some sense of self-determination in an otherwise unpredictable abusive environment, thus becoming a stable part of that alter's/ego state's behavioral repertoire. The therapist must be firm and unequivocal in setting limits on sexual and aggressive behavior, but must avoid punishing or rejecting the alter/ego state engaging in that behavior.

As with resistance, Putnam (1989) cautions against therapeutic preoccupation with transference phenomena, urging instead interpretation and focus upon transference only as it impedes treatment. This stance prevents the client from successfully avoiding the difficult work of therapy by presenting repeated transference distortions, keeping the treatment on track and allowing minor transference problems to resolve naturally as therapy unfolds. The distorted perception that accompanies transference will not yield to rational disputation, but will respond to patient, supportive exploration of meanings and their experiential origins.

A number of factors contribute to the strong countertransferences experienced by therapists. Certainly the complexity and intensity of the therapeutic work creates a high level of demand upon the therapist. The ongoing stress of this demand can manifest in heightened reactivity to client behavior; the therapist may be apprehensive or irritable, or in other ways add to the strain experienced by the hypervigilant client. Tension and uncertainty in the therapist will generally magnify the threat experienced by alters and interfere with treatment progress. The therapist may be avoidant of dealing with the client's traumatic experience and abreactive distress, colluding with the client's natural resistance to this painful work.

Every therapist has personal preferences for certain personality characteristics, and dislike of others. Because these characteristics (e.g., dependency, aggressivity, affectivity, impulsivity, rigidity, etc.) will be expressed in extreme forms by different alters/ego states, the therapist is quite vulnerable to developing strong differential reactions to alters/ego states, which will create destabilizing and destructive effects in the client. Therapists inevitably find that dissociative clients experience therapeutic detachment or neutrality as rejection. This reaction requires the effective therapist to participate in a real relationship with the client in a collaborative approach to the treatment. Although honesty and directness by the therapist are essential, the needs of the client must determine therapeutic choices and behavior. This means that the therapist must monitor and contain his or her personal preferences. He or she must retain a professional respect and acknowledgement of all alters/ego states based upon a sophisticated appreciation of the experiential origins and systemic functions of all components of the dissociated personality.

Because of the intensity of the dissociative client's distress and the severity of his or her early abuse, the therapist is at risk of identifying with the despair and hopelessness voiced by the client. Kluft (1989a) has identified this as a contributing factor to the therapist's demoralization in treating MPD. The effective therapist will strike a balance between strong empathic sensitivity to the distress of the client and professional objectivity. This balance allows the therapist to serve as a positive and helpful resource, rather than sharing the pain experienced by the client.

For further consideration of transference and countertransference in work with MPD patients, see Beahrs (1982), Greaves (1988), Kluft (1989a, 1989c), Putnam (1989), and Wilbur (1988).

The Treatment Process. The treatment of dissociative disorder is progressive, with an overarching linear direction toward the integration of the client's behavioral and psychological functioning. The steps that lead toward this goal are (a) establishing initial rapport and trust; (b) making the diagnosis and informing the client; (c) establishing communication with alters/ego states; (d) developing an understanding of the function and structure of the dissociative system; (e) working with the problems of particular alters/ego states while helping the client develop increased coordination, cooperation, and integration of current function among alters/ego states; (f) helping the client develop nondissociative coping skills; (g) confronting the dissociative process and supporting the client's integration of memory, affect, and identity via abreaction of traumatic experience; and (h) helping the client develop and consolidate new patterns of identity, psychological function, and behavior (Bloch, 1989; Braun, 1986b).

This sequence may create a false impression of simplicity. In fact, the development of trust, the establishment of relationship with alters, and the revision of comprehension of the dissociative structure as alters emerge in the treatment are all likely to continue almost to the completion of successful therapy. The host and various other alters often will display denial of multiplicity recurrently throughout treatment. Also, the occurrence of significant stress in therapy and in the natural environment often will result in the client's regression into further dissociation and sometimes leads to the formation of new alters or fragments. As these developments unfold, they must be addressed before further progress can take place. The provision of support must replace further confrontation whenever the client or alters/ego states show signs of being overwhelmed by affect or stress.

Cooperation, Integration, and Unification. As internal cooperation and increased teamwork develops among alters/ego states, the disruptions of functioning attributable to intrapsychic conflict will diminish even as memory, affect, and identity remain dissociated. The integration of these aspects of personality must be preceded by abreactive working-through of traumatic experience, which makes possible the blending of alters/ego states and the diffusion of dissociative barriers. Late in therapy, there may be signs or client reports of spontaneous fusion of alters/ego states, signaling readiness for personality unification. This process typically occurs in a stepwise manner, with two or more alters/ego states combining at a time. Alter fusion requires a consolidation period of support as this newly formed psychological entity becomes acclimated to its new identity and experience. Successful fusion will not result from therapist pressure toward that end. Such pressure will typically lead to either compliant suppression of overt signs of dissociation or the client's flight from treatment. When the client is ready for fusion, he or she will require at most a therapeutic ritual of joining; Kluft (1982) and Putnam (1989) provide discussions of fusion rituals.

Therapeutic fusions often will fail to be maintained, and the client then will experience reseparation of alters. When this occurs, both therapist and client must understand that, rather than indicating failure or inadequacy of the client, failed fusion simply means that more therapeutic work will be required before successful fusion can realistically be expected to take place

(Kluft, 1986a). The therapist's rejection of the notion that fusion is the *sine qua non* of successful treatment is the best way to prevent premature and inevitably unsuccessful fusion. The final unification of personality can occur only through the stable fusion of all alters and the development of a stable new identity capable of managing the demands of life without a relapse to dissociative coping strategies.

The terms "fusion," "integration," and "unification" are defined differently by different writers. Kluft (1988b) draws the following distinction: Integration is the general process of the client's reduced reliance upon the dissociative segregation of experience, fusion is the absence of signs of MPD for 3 continuous months (herein also referring to the stable blending of two or more alters), and unification is the blending of alters into a single nondissociative personality structure. Drawing upon the meaning of integration in race relations, and consistent with the usage of Beahrs (1982) and the Watkinses (J. G. Watkins & H. H. Watkins, 1981), an alternative definition of integration involves increased harmonious, respectful, cooperative, and effective coexistence of the various aspects and components of the client's personality structure. Even when this degree of success is realized, there may be continued maintenance of separate identities and discriminable experience; when the relatively well-integrated client no longer seeks dividedness, fusion and unification will follow. Kluft (1984c, 1986a, 1988b) observes that MPD clients whose treatment results in fusion and unification generally fare better than those who stop short of that goal. Nevertheless, many dissociative clients will not be inclined toward or capable of unification, but may still benefit greatly from treatment aimed at improved functional integration. Therapeutic success is relative in this as in all forms of mental health treatment.

It is easy for therapists to become preoccupied with the alter structure of MPD, and to share the client's subjective reality that alters are "different people." However, alters and ego states are the client's internal representations of unintegrated object relations and it is these object relations that become integrated in effective treatment, rather than a merging of separate people into a single person. As previously dissociated self-representations, object representations, affects, impulses, memories, and behavioral repertoires become integrated, the subjective reality of the client is transformed. This transformation includes alteration of the perceived identities that have previously been experienced as separate and discriminable. Greaves (1989) provides an illuminating discussion of the integrative process, precursors of integration, and indicators that treatment is not moving in a positive direction.

The integrative process creates distress for the client, both the pain of reowning traumatic or threatening experience and the distress that accompanies massive change in one's experience of self and the world. The coming together of experience generally precipitates emotional and behavioral crisis in the client, which requires careful monitoring, pacing, and support by the therapist.

The successful unification of personality is not the end point of MPD treatment, but simply another milestone. Kluft (1988b) and Putnam (1989) both emphasize the importance of post-unification treatment, which focuses upon support and consolidation of therapeutic gains, the enhancement of nondissociative coping skills, and the stabilization of the new structure of identity, affect, and behavior as the client approaches the difficulties of life as a novice. Kluft (1988b) wryly comments that "the cure of multiple personality disorder leaves the patient afflicted with single personality disorder, the state in which most patients seek psychotherapy" (p. 225).

Realistic Expectations and Prognosis. Much remains to be learned about prediction of outcome in the treatment of dissociative disorder. It is clear that in the absence of correct diagnosis and appropriate therapy, these clients tend to respond poorly to professional treatment and remain quite dysfunctional. Only recently, however, has acceptance and knowledge of these disorders progressed to the point where sufficiently large numbers of cases and skilled therapists can be identified to enable careful attention to questions of outcome and prognosis.

Based upon clinical experience, Caul (1988) has suggested several pragmatic questions pertaining to prognosis: (a) Does the client accept the MPD diagnosis? (Rejection of the diagnosis prevents the establishment of an effective therapeutic relationship.); (b) Has the client received prior lengthy treatment of MPD, with several therapists? (Difficult, lengthy treatment and therapist changes, other than for geographical reasons, bode poorly for treatment outcome.); (c) How many alters are present? (The more alters, the longer and more difficult treatment will be.); (d) Is the client committed to defining alters as separate people, using dissociation as a preferred means of coping, and relying upon alters to continue to hold trauma and solve problems? (These behaviors indicate unwillingness to give up dissociation.); (e) Does the client dominate the course of therapy and the therapist? (This pattern augurs poorly for the process and outcome of treatment.); (f) Is it difficult to contract with the client? (An uncooperative, unreliable client makes effective therapy impossible.); (g) Does the client engage in extensive confabulation and the construction of reports which are inconsistent with actual experience? (This suggests a dysfunctional reliance upon fantasy, deception, and self-deception.); (h) Is there extreme violence in behavior or attitude? (Is the extreme violence unresponsive to treatment?); and (i) Is the client more focused upon uncovering than upon resolution of dissociation?

Kluft (1986a) has identified several factors suggesting negative outcome of MPD treatment: the strong resistance of alters to giving up their separate identities, a high degree of masochism, and severe personality disorder concurrent with dissociation. Coons (1986) found that continuing retraumatization during therapy prevents integration.

Even among highly experienced and expert therapists, there remain a number of different perspectives regarding prognosis and outcome, and it will probably be some time before consensus can be reached. Despite Kluft's generally optimistic view of this issue, it is clear that many MPD clients have been so severely traumatized at such an early point in ego development that significant personality integration will simply be impossible. Many clients are so deeply committed to their dissociative defenses and to their MPD identity that fusion is out of the question; these clients will require either continuous or episodic treatment throughout their life in order to optimize their functional adaptation and coping.

EGO-STATE THERAPY

The writings of John and Helen Watkins (J. G. Watkins, 1978; J. G. Watkins & H. H. Watkins, 1979, 1981, 1984, 1988) and Beahrs (1982, 1983) emphasize the dissociative continuum and the therapeutic goal of increased harmony, communication, and cooperation among alters/ego states in MPD and ESD, rather than fusion and unification of personality. This focus is a natural outgrowth of the observation that varying degrees of personality dissociation are normally observed among people and that only severe dissociation impedes effective adjustment and coping. In fact, the complexity and contradictory demands of life require the processes of discrimination and generalization to be balanced for effective psychological functioning; it is the process of discrimination which, in extreme forms, gives rise to dissociative disorder. Homogeneous and heterogeneous experiencing occur in a flexible dialectic relationship in a person's construction of internal representations that can approximate the complexity of the real world and thereby generate relatively successful adaptive behavior. When that relationship is altered by dissociative processes, the normal integration of internal representations, experience, affect, and behavior is impaired.

Ego-state therapy seeks to identify and articulate the conflicting perceptions, motives, affects, intentions, and behaviors of different ego states within the dissociative client. This discrimination of ego-state-specific material is typically facilitated by the use of hypnosis, which allows the isolation of ego states from the ongoing flow of psychological functioning. Enactment techniques (e.g., "two-chair" work, amplification of affect, internal dialogue, etc.) are also employed to differentiate ego states. As conflicts between ego states are explored, the role of these conflicts in creating symptoms of emotional distress, somatic distress, and behavioral dysfunction becomes clear. The therapist then serves as a mediator between conflictual ego states, striving to improve internal communication, conflict resolution, and compromise. The goal of therapy is a synthesis of new styles of internal diplomacy that allows increased acceptance of the disparate motivations and specialized functions of various ego states.

The therapist models and encourages validation of each ego state, while seeking to help the client develop enhanced internal cooperation in solving problems and managing affect. Ego states are urged to forego acting out in favor of increased tolerance and support of each other's legitimate roles and functions. A strong values emphasis is present in this form of therapy, promoting the preference of "partnership" over adversarial styles of internal relations. No ego states are dismissed or rejected in reaching solutions to conflicts, and the therapist repeatedly suggests that since no ego state can possibly be eliminated, the development of peaceful co-existence is the only strategy that can lead to satisfactory adjustment. In addition to this emphasis upon improved relations between ego states, treatment also focuses upon resolving the particular problems, distresses, distortions, and impairments of individual ego states. The intense, unmodulated affects, dysfunctional attitudes, and developmentally immature misattributions expressed by ego states are explored and modified.

Repetition compulsions, self-defeating behaviors and expectancies, and fantasy-based perceptions are confronted.

THE USE OF HYPNOSIS IN TREATMENT

A close relationship has been observed between naturally occurring dissociation and hypnotic phenomena (Beahrs, 1982; Bliss, 1986; E. Hilgard, 1977); this has led to the view that hypnosis is a structured and interactive form of dissociation, and dissociation is a form of autohypnosis. The use of hypnosis in treating dissociative disorder provides a valuable and effective modality, but it is not magical and must be carefully thought through. Hypnosis should never be employed without a clearly articulated rationale.

Dissociative clients are almost always excellent hypnotic subjects, capable of developing extremely deep levels of hypnotic trance. They have used dissociation for years and have developed strong skills for changing states of consciousness. However, some clients will resist entering the hypnotic state out of fear of loss of control, fear of being controlled by the therapist, or reluctance to allow probing of the dissociative system. The therapist's suggestion of the positive value of hypnosis to the client's treatment should generally be postponed until initial rapport has been developed. A patient and supportive discussion of hypnosis and the client's reactions to its use should precede the first induction. These clients will generally respond to simple, direct induction procedures and will often be able to learn to enter trance rapidly in response to cue words that have become associated with hypnotic experience in session. Dissociative clients tend to respond poorly to indirect Ericksonian inductions due to their sensitivity to manipulative interactions.

Hypnosis is useful in several different aspects of treatment: (a) developing therapeutic rapport, (b) accessing alters/ego states, (c) managing affect and behavior, (d) dismantling amnesic barriers, (e) resolving internal conflicts, (f) restoring integrative processes, (g) supporting abreaction, (h) developing nondissociative coping skills, and (i) blending or integrating personality functioning. The range of specific hypnotic interventions is limited only by the therapist's creativity and facility in employing hypnosis and his or her understanding of dissociation.

Therapeutic rapport is augmented by the induction of hypnosis, which establishes a collaborative and supportive pattern of interaction whereby the therapist leads the client toward relief from distress. Hypnotic relaxation, creation of a "perfect place" or sanctuary via hypnotic imagery, hypnotically induced "sleep" for rest and relief from acute distress, hypnotic anesthesia/analgesia, and hypnotic ego strengthening are among the relief-producing hypnotic interventions that can help the client respond to the therapist in a trusting and receptive manner.

Accessing alters/ego states through hypnosis simply involves asking for the emergence of a particular alter/ego state (e.g., "I'd like to speak with the person or part that holds depression; if that part is willing to speak with me, please signify by raising the first finger of the right hand") or extending an open invitation for any alter/ego state to emerge. Hypnotic switching enables the client to develop order in internal interaction and to avoid the unease that often accompanies spontaneous switching. "Traffic control" by the therapist can establish a coherence to internal processing that the client has never before experienced, thereby facilitating the client's acceptance of alters/ego states and their concerns.

Hypnosis allows the therapist's management of the client's extreme affect and acting-out behavior. The therapist first inquires about the meanings, causes, and purposes of affect or impulse. Then he or she attempts to reduce the intensity of those feelings by support, ventilation, cognitive restructuring, suggestion, or seeking assistance and nurturance of distressed alters/ego states by others. Hypnotic sleep for acting-out alters/ego states or those in acute distress can be induced if other efforts are unproductive. In order to minimize system disruption and suppression, this should be done benevolently, with explicit rejection of punitive intentions, and should be time-limited (e.g., "And now the suicidal one will slip down into a deep, restful sleep, below the level of pain, and will remain asleep until the next session").

Alters/ego states can be taught affect modulation through the hypnotic creation of internal affect containers that will hold unmanageable levels of affect, allowing the experiencing of more moderate intensities of feeling. The control that this creates helps the client build self-esteem, a sense of self-efficacy, and confidence in his or her coping ability. Attempts to simply eliminate distress and impulse will be ineffective and will contribute to denial. Conversely, interventions that modify the client's experience of distress or impulse will lessen the rigidity of dysfunctional patterns of affect and expression.

Hypnotherapy is a valuable tool for helping the client dismantle amnesic and dissociative barriers in a gradual, tolerable, paced manner. When conversing with alters/ego states, the therapist can instruct the host and/or others to attend and remain aware of the conversation, "bringing back to your waking consciousness only as much as you can manage." Age regression and suggestion of recall are useful means of enhancing memory retrieval, always to be used with care lest intolerable experiences be recalled. Interactions among several or all alters can be orchestrated, to aid the process of integration of memory and functioning. In order to reduce the risk of overwhelming the client's defenses, these dismantling strategies should be reserved until therapy is progressing well and considerable ego strengthening has taken place.

Internal conflicts often can be resolved via hypnotic interventions that help alters/ego states develop skills at self-expression and receptive interaction among themselves. Internal committees, conferences, and governance procedures can be developed to provide a structure for partnership and collaborative problem solving. As alters/ego states gradually engage more with each other, their isolations and antagonisms will gradually yield to greater integration of experiences.

The abreactive component of treatment is difficult for client and therapist alike; this component can be structured and managed most effectively by judicious hypnotic intervention. Hypnotic revivification of traumatic experiences allows for control of the process, reducing the risk of retraumatization and destabilization of the client. Helen Watkins (1980) has developed a "silent abreaction" hypnotic procedure that allows the internal ventilation of intense affect without external expression. "Screen" techniques involve the hypnotized client revivifying traumatic sequences on an imaged screen, with controls for managing the intensity and pace of the experience. Each therapist will modify established techniques and develop new ones to respond to the idiosyncratic features of each client and each abreaction.

Hypnosis supports the client's development of nondissociative coping skills in a variety of ways. The client or particular alters/ego states can be induced to rehearse increasingly self-assertive and self-promoting behavior in hypnotic imagery prior to implementation, and to employ hypnotic calming and affect management skills *in vivo*. Alters/ego states can be urged to "share time" (to participate in co-executive experiencing and behavior), first in the hypnotic state and then in "real time." The client or particular alters/ego states can be taught to use trance to consider alternative approaches to problems or situations and to anticipate likely outcomes of different strategies to improve problem-solving skills.

Hypnotic rituals of fusing, blending, or unifying alters can be helpful in structuring that process, once the client has progressed to that point and indicated an acceptance of that outcome. As Putnam (1989) states, the nature of the fusion process is not well understood at this point, but seems often to be facilitated by formal hypnotic ritual in the treatment of MPD.

The therapist planning to use hypnosis should review the following resources for a broader perspective: Allison (1984); Bliss (1986); Braun (1984a, 1984b); Caul (1978); Horevitz (1983); Kluft (1982, 1983, 1986a); Putnam (1989); D. Spiegel (1989); and H. H. Watkins (1980).

PHARMACOTHERAPY

It is commonly understood that chemotherapy has no therapeutic effect upon the dissociative process, and is generally accompanied by complex, unpredictable, idiosyncratic and negative side effects. One of the fascinating aspects of MPD is that alters are affected differently by medications, leading to reactions that are difficult to manage. Psychotropic agents administered to manage specific focal symptoms in MPD clients are likely to cause secondary responses that may be more problematic than the target symptoms. Many MPD clients report extremely negative experiences with medication prescribed to reduce such symptoms. An appropriately conservative strategy is to avoid medicating symptoms unless they are so disabling or risky that to withhold medication would jeopardize the client's welfare. Even in those instances, the response to pharmacotherapy must be monitored closely and continuously, with discontinuation or modification of the regimen as soon as untoward effects are observed. Because MPD invariably leads to discontinuity of experience, these clients generally encounter difficulties complying with drug-administration regimens, and must be continuously monitored for over- and underadministration of any prescribed medicines.

Antipsychotics often are selected in response to such symptoms as hallucinations, disorganization, and agitation. Although a brief positive sedative response may accompany brief, low-dosage use of these agents at times of acute agitation, continued administration or the use of normal therapeutic doses will typically not be beneficial. The suppression of alters with these drugs often results in further dissociation or later rebound agitation and acting out by those alters. Child alters may become disoriented and traumatized by the use of antipsychotics.

It is generally found that antidepressants may be helpful occasionally, but only if significant depression is noted throughout the dissociative system rather than being confined to a single alter or a small number of alters. Anecdotally, antidepressants and mood elevators at times serve to disinhibit acting-out alters and reduce the system's control over aggressive or impulsive alters. Monoamine oxidase inhibitors (MAOIs) should be avoided due to the risk of tyramine sabotage.

Anxiolytics are often useful in the brief control of acute anxiety, panic, and agitation, but like antidepressants may serve as a "releaser" of acting-out alters. A diminishing of positive response is generally observed with long-term use of anxiolytics, as with other medications, and these drugs carry great potential for abuse. Equivocal results have been reported regarding the effectiveness of anticonvulsants in controlling acting out and instability in MPD patients.

MPD clients typically encounter difficulties with anesthesia for surgery, with some alters either not becoming anesthetized or the system requiring dangerously high doses of anesthetic before total anesthesia is achieved. Hypnotic anesthesia is often helpful, wherein the client is trained that all alters but one will descend into deep hypnotic sleep prior to administration of the anesthetic, with the executive alter or host experiencing the chemical anesthetic during surgery, and providing a cue to other alters to resume their normal consciousness once safely returned to recovery.

MPD clients will often seek and often abuse analgesics to relieve headache and acute psychogenic pain. These drugs generally are ineffective with MPD clients, and hypnotic procedures typically will be more effective.

For a more thorough discussion of the pharmacotherapy of MPD, consult Barkin, Braun, and Kluft (1986), Putnam (1989), and Ross (1989). Nonphysician therapists will find it valuable to develop a cooperative relationship with a psychiatrist who is willing to manage medication on a referral/consultation basis, perhaps providing copies of relevant literature if the psychiatrist is unfamiliar with MPD.

HOSPITALIZATION

Although the primary modality of treatment for MPD and ESD is outpatient psychotherapy, it is not uncommon for these clients periodically to require and benefit from brief psychiatric hospitalization. Given current economic constraints (reduced subsidized hospital care, increased preauthorization controls, and limits on duration of hospital care by third parties), a number of nonclinical factors impact upon the decision to hospitalize. The nonphysician therapist may also face the problems of not having staff authority to admit and manage the care of his or her clients in the hospital setting and having to rely upon cooperative relations with psychiatrist colleagues in order to effect a successful hospital stay. Hospitalization that is not coordinated by the client's primary therapist will at best be less productive than otherwise possible. At worst, an uncoordinated hospital stay can cause additional trauma to the client due to the use of treatment approaches that are inconsistent with the overall therapy plan.

A major factor in the success or failure of the inpatient care of dissociative clients is the attitude of the hospital staff toward dissociative dysfunction. A skeptical staff is likely to see the MPD patient as borderline or manipulative, which often results in controlling or punitive behavior toward the patient. However, a staff that has been oriented, trained, and supervised in the treatment of these disorders can provide effective and skillful care that contributes to a positive patient response to the hospital and a beneficial treatment result. The therapist who is sensitive to this issue will provide literature, consultation, and training (e.g., discussing anticipated problems) to hospital staff involved in the care of dissociative patients. Ideally, one highly skilled member of the nursing staff for each shift will be identified as the coordinator of care for the dissociative patient, managing the contributions of other staff and serving as liaison between the psychiatrist or other primary therapist and hospital staff, as well as insuring the provision of rational, consistent service to the patient.

MPD patients often create many problems in the hospital. Staff splitting is common, in response to the variable behaviors of the patient's alters and the intense countertransferences manifested by the staff. Other patients generally react negatively to the behavior of MPD patients, resenting the great amount of attention that they receive from staff. Confusing and disruptive tensions surface, generating stress within the relatively closed system of the hospital unit and interfering with the maintenance of a supportive structured environment for patient care.

These problems must be anticipated and managed by unit supervisors, with an emphasis upon maintaining open, clear communication and collaborative effort among all care providers. All staff should be advised to monitor their own subjective reactions particularly closely, in order to anticipate and contain acting out in response to the complexities, difficulties, and frustrations inherent in treating MPD in an inpatient setting. Regular scheduled meetings of the treatment team should include attention to the effects of the client's treatment upon the members of the team and their relationships among themselves.

There are several indicators for hospitalization: (a) acute suicide risk or engagement in uncontrolled destructive or self-destructive behavior, (b) acute distress that the client cannot manage as an outpatient, or (c) the need for security and access to physical restraints in order to pursue abreaction or direct contact with alters that are anticipated to be physically dangerous. Hospitalization periods should be used for safety and containment, but also should provide an opportunity to engage in therapeutic work that might destabilize the patient's adaptation if conducted on an outpatient basis. Attention should be directed toward working with alters to resolve the internal disruptions that created the need for hospitalization. Physical restraint during therapeutic elicitation of assaultive alters should be used only if hypnotic restraints are insufficient to contain the behavior of those alters. The patient should be carefully prepared for the intensity of this type of work, after agreeing to the use of restraints. The therapist should be mindful that the use of physical restraint often will trigger strong disturbances and abreactions of traumatic experiences. Nevertheless, some alters cannot be elicited safely without restraint due to the intensity of their affect and impulse. Avoidance of the necessary treatment work with these alters will generally result in eventual volatile and risky acting out.

Whenever possible, MPD patients should have private rooms, in order to have privacy and freedom from the complicating effects of other patients' behavior (and vice versa). Milieu treatment is not a major component of most MPD treatment plans; MPD patients' dealings with other psychiatric patients may be unsatisfying and problematic. Participation in group psychotherapy and other social therapies generally will not be helpful, although individualized expressive therapies often can be quite positive and valuable components of coordinated inpatient treatment. Various alters will test limits and act out their feelings about being hospitalized; hospital policies, rules, and procedures should be carefully explained and consistently enforced.

For more detailed discussions of hospital treatment, see: Kluft (1984a, 1984c); Putnam (1989); Ross (1989); Sakheim et al. (1988); and Young (1986).

THE CHILD CLIENT

MPD and ESD are childhood-onset conditions, but typically have not been identified and treated until the client has achieved young adulthood. This will certainly change as greater professional attention is drawn to dissociative disorder and the sequelae of childhood trauma. Invariably, the dissociation and formation of the first alter/ego state occurs in early childhood, correlating with the child's normal developmental propensity toward fantasy generation (Young, 1988a). The coalescence of an "imaginary friend" into a well-defined identity is common in the natural history of MPD, and "inner child" alters/ego states are present in all cases of ESD and MPD.

Childhood dissociative conditions have been referred to as "incipient MPD," which correctly suggests that these dissociative structures are formative and less clearly defined and elaborated than later forms. Consequently, it is commonly held that the treatment of dissociative children is easier and more rapid than the treatment of adult MPD when adequate environmental structure and protection from further traumatization is possible. The child's return to a traumatizing environment will lead inevitably to a resumption of dissociative processes. Once dissociation is successfully employed as a defense, it becomes a preferred means of coping with threat.

The diagnostic difficulties encountered with adult dissociative disorder are compounded in child and adolescent presentations. Not only do these clients invariably satisfy diagnostic criteria for various Axis I diagnoses, but also the features that are uniquely dissociative often are difficult to identify and to differentiate from normal developmental phenomena (e.g., the confusion between fantasy and reality in younger children, mood alteration in adolescents).

The identification of recurrent sexual abuse, physical abuse, incest, or other significant traumatization (severe childhood illness, ear infection, burns, witnessing of violence, etc.) should

80

alert the clinician to look for dissociative process, and the trans-generational transmission of abuse and dissociation (Braun, 1985; Coons, 1985) makes it important to evaluate the children of known MPD clients for dissociative disorder. A number of other signs and symptoms combine to suggest dissociative defense in children, including amnesia, auditory hallucinations, significant variation in mood or behavior, significant variation in ability or school performance, denial of awareness of events known to have been witnessed, passive-influence phenomena, trance-like phenomena, a reputation of being a liar, sporadic depression, sporadic behavioral regression, inappropriate sexual behavior, and frequent confusion. The diagnostic process requires patience, trust, and support and should be conducted separately from legally related assessment of child abuse allegations. The clinician must be comfortable with identifying the range of dissociative presentations, because child and adolescent clients are not as marked in their dissociative characteristics as adult clients.

Treatment of child and adolescent clients may involve play therapy, hypnotic techniques, and integration-seeking talk therapy. Abreaction of traumatic experience often is less disturbing than in adults, presumably because crystallization of the representations of trauma does not occur in child clients. Fusion/unification of personality processes and identity is more likely in younger dissociative clients because alters are not firmly differentiated and have not developed narcissistic investment in separateness. Successful treatment must be highly supportive and must include work with parents/caretakers to insure protection and safety for the client.

For further information on the diagnosis and treatment of dissociative disorder in children and adolescents, see: Bowman, Blix, and Coons (1985); Braun (1985); Coons (1985); Fagan and McMahon (1984); Kluft (1984b, 1985a, 1985c, 1986b); and Kluft, Braun, and Sachs (1985).

EFFECTS OF TREATMENT UPON THE TREATER

Professional engagement with clients presenting MPD or ESD is widely recognized to impact heavily upon the clinician. A number of adjectives capture the nature of this work: complex, baffling, frustrating, draining, frightening, fascinating, engrossing, enlightening, and consuming. Therapists generally become fascinated with dissociative phenomena upon initial identification of

MPD or ESD in a client. This fascination can later yield to demoralization as this difficult treatment drags on (Kluft, 1989a). Additionally, those who speak openly with colleagues about their experience with these disorders often encounter skepticism or ridicule; in many communities, they will feel quite isolated if no supportive colleagues are available.

Most therapists working in this area find that their experience with dissociation transforms the understanding of many clinical presentations. The enthusiastic clinician will begin to identify dissociative features in many clients, often correctly and sometimes incorrectly. Keeping one's professional bearings in the face of the demands of this work requires sound clinical judgment, specialized training, review of the literature, consultation, and supervision.

Careful attention to establishing and maintaining reasonable boundaries in the therapeutic relationship is the therapist's best defense against excessive stress and burnout in working with these clients. The level of disturbance, need, and complexity that the therapist encounters with these clients leads to the risk of "playing rescuer" and assuming complete responsibility for the client's welfare and survival. This error, which will lead to a sense of being overwhelmed and a loss of professional balance, is countered by continuous scrutiny, with supervision, of one's countertransference and of the direction of treatment. Realistic expectations of the client and the therapy will facilitate the therapist's development of a sound perspective from which to view the work. The therapist must avoid letting this engaging therapy dominate his or her life, by maintaining a stable balance between professional and personal priorities, responsibilities, and gratifications.

The well-grounded therapist will tolerate frequent bewilderment, confusion, and uncertainty; one must accept the inevitability of therapeutic error (Greaves, 1988) while striving to correct such errors. Persistent, patient therapeutic effort and attention ultimately will reveal the information that is needed to resolve uncertainty and confusion. Therapist error generally will result in little damage if it is quickly identified, discussed, and corrected. Despite their frequent instability and continuous vulnerability, dissociative clients have survived severe ongoing threats to their physical and psychological survival, and are unlikely to be destroyed by unwitting error. Often the inner self-helper (ISH) or other helpful alter will alert the therapist to errors and misunderstandings and serve as a valuable advisor on getting the therapy back on track.

Therapy of MPD and ESD often will present the therapist with moments of fear due to the intense affect, impulse, and acting-out behavior that is part of these conditions. Kluft (1983), J. G. Watkins (1984), J. G. Watkins and H. H. Watkins (1988), Putnam (1989), and others have provided guidance for the management of crises. Nevertheless, the therapist must possess a high level of confidence in his or her clinical skills and resourcefulness in order to handle these crises with relative comfort and grace. The safety of both therapist and client is always the first priority; psychotherapy cannot proceed under conditions of significant risk and must yield to efforts to re-establish security.

Therapists often find that continuous exposure to client accounts and revivifications of severe brutalization and traumatization leads to what has been referred to as "secondary posttraumatic stress disorder," a demoralization and blunting of the therapist's emotional response. The best prevention against secondary PTSD is the maintenance of solid ego boundaries to prevent the client's pain and disturbance from becoming "contagious," with open ventilation of one's own reactions in supervision or support-seeking dialogue with professional peers.

SUMMARY

This monograph has presented an introduction to the complex and demanding processes of identification, diagnosis, assessment, and treatment of dissociative disorder. The clinician embarking on professional work with these disorders should be well aware of the rigors and difficulties of this work, seeking specialty training, literature immersion, and supervision. Dissociative disorders, although serious and disabling, are eminently treatable. Most dissociative clients are capable of resolving their dysfunction and distress, in part or completely, and can experience a marked improvement in their quality of life. Despite the difficulties, clinical work in this area is highly rewarding and the clinician can expect to experience considerable personal and professional growth in exchange for the effort expended in treating these clients.

Understanding dissociative processes will add immeasurably to the professional's comprehension of basic human coping behavior and appreciation of the strengths and abilities of all persons, even in the face of overwhelming trauma. Clinical involvement in this area of practice will certainly lead to the expansion of professional sophistication and confidence in working with all forms of psychological distress and dysfunction.

APPENDIX

ORGANIZATION

International Society for the Study of Multiple Personality and Dissociation, 5700 Old Orchard Road, First Floor, Skokie, IL 60077-1024. Telephone: (708) 966-4322. (Contact for information about membership, referrals to members, affiliated local study groups and societies, and the Fall International Conference.)

NEWSLETTERS

Many Voices, P.O. Box 2639, Cincinnati, OH 45201-2639. (This is a newsletter by and for multiple personality disorder clients. Cost: $30 in U.S., $36 elsewhere; bi-monthly.)

MPD Reaching Out, c/o Public Relations Department, Royal Ottawa Hospital, 1145 Carling Avenue, Ottawa, Ontario, Canada K1Z 7K4. (A Canadian newsletter by and for MPD clients.)

Trauma and Recovery, Department of Psychiatry and Behavioral Sciences, Akron General Medical Center, 400 Wabash Avenue, Akron, OH 43407. Telephone: (216) 384-6525. (This is a newsletter of the Ohio Society for the Study of Multiple Personality and Dissociation.)

JOURNAL

Dissociation, c/o Ridgeview Institute, 3995 South Cobb Drive, Smyrna, GA 30080. Telephone: (800) 345-9775. (This is the journal of the International Society for the Study of Multiple Personality and Dissociation.)

REFERENCES

Abrams, J. (Ed.). (1990). *Reclaiming the Inner Child*. Los Angeles: Tarcher.

Allison, R. B. (1974). A new treatment approach for multiple personalities. *American Journal of Clinical Hypnosis, 17,* 15-32.

Allison, R. B. (1980). *Minds in Many Pieces*. New York: Rawson, Wade.

Allison, R. B. (1984). Difficulties diagnosing the multiple personality syndrome in a death penalty case. *International Journal of Clinical and Experimental Hypnosis, 32,* 102-117.

American Psychiatric Association. (1980). *Diagnostic and Statistical Manual of Mental Disorders* (3rd ed.). Washington, DC: Author.

American Psychiatric Association. (1987). *Diagnostic and Statistical Manual of Mental Disorders* (3rd ed. rev.). Washington, DC: Author.

Assagioli, R. (1965). *Psychosynthesis: A Manual of Principles and Techniques*. New York: Hobbs & Dorman.

Barkin, R., Braun, B. G., & Kluft, R. P. (1986). The dilemma of drug treatment for multiple personality disorder. In B. G. Braun (Ed.), *Treatment of Multiple Personality Disorder* (pp. 107-132). Washington, DC: American Psychiatric Press.

Bass, E., & Davis, L. (1988). *The Courage to Heal*. New York: Harper & Row.

Beahrs, J. O. (1982). *Unity and Multiplicity: Multilevel Consciousness of Self in Hypnosis, Psychiatric Disorder and Mental Health*. New York: Brunner/Mazel.

Beahrs, J. O. (1983). Co-consciousness: A common denominator in hypnosis, multiple personality, and normalcy. *American Journal of Clinical Hypnosis, 26,* 100-113.

Berne, E. (1961). *Transactional Analysis in Psychotherapy.* New York: Grove Press.

Bernstein, E. M., & Putnam, F. W. (1986). Development, reliability, and validity of a dissociation scale. *Journal of Nervous and Mental Disease, 174,* 727-735.

Bjornson, L., Reagor, P. A., & Kasten, J. D. (1988, October). *Multiple Personality Patterns on Standardized Psychological Tests.* Paper presented at Fifth International Conference on Multiple Personality and Dissociative States, Chicago, IL.

Bliss, E. L. (1986). *Multiple Personality, Allied Disorders and Hypnosis.* New York: Oxford.

Bloch, J. P. (1988). Clinical assessment of multiple personality and dissociation. In P. A. Keller & S. R. Heyman (Eds.), *Innovations in Clinical Practice: A Source Book* (Vol. 7, pp. 113-125). Sarasota, FL: Professional Resource Exchange.

Bloch, J. P. (1989). Treatment of multiple personality and dissociative disorder. In P. A. Keller & S. R. Heyman (Eds.), *Innovations in Clinical Practice: A Source Book* (Vol. 8, pp. 55-67). Sarasota, FL: Professional Resource Exchange.

Bowlby, J. (1980). *Loss: Sadness and Depression.* New York: Basic Books.

Bowman, R. R., Blix, S., & Coons, P. M. (1985). Multiple personality in adolescence: Relationship to incestual experiences. *Journal of the American Academy of Child Psychiatry, 24,* 109-114.

Bradshaw, J. (1988). *Healing the Shame That Binds You.* Deerfield Beach, FL: Health Communications.

Braun, B. G. (1983a). Neurophysiologic changes in multiple personality due to integration: A preliminary report. *American Journal of Clinical Hypnosis, 26,* 84-92.

Braun, B. G. (1983b). Psychophysiologic phenomena in multiple personality and hypnosis. *American Journal of Clinical Hypnosis, 26,* 124-137.

Braun, B. G. (1984a). Hypnosis creates multiple personality. Myth or reality? *International Journal of Clinical and Experimental Hypnosis, 32,* 191-197.

Braun, B. G. (1984b). Uses of hypnosis with multiple personality. *Psychiatric Annals, 14,* 34-40.

Braun, B. G. (1985). The transgenerational incidence of dissociation and multiple personality disorder: A preliminary report.

In R. P. Kluft (Ed.), *Childhood Antecedents of Multiple Personality* (pp. 127-150). Washington, DC: American Psychiatric Press.

Braun, B. G. (Ed.). (1986a). *Treatment of Multiple Personality Disorder.* Washington, DC: American Psychiatric Press.

Braun, B. G. (1986b). Issues in the psychotherapy of multiple personality disorder. In B. G. Braun (Ed.), *Treatment of Multiple Personality Disorder* (pp. 1-28). Washington, DC: American Psychiatric Press.

Braun, B. G. (1988a). The BASK (Behavior, affect, sensation, knowledge) model of dissociation. *Dissociation, 1*(1), 4-23.

Braun, B. G. (1988b). The BASK model of dissociation: Clinical applications. *Dissociation, 1*(2), 16-23.

Braun, B. G., & Sachs, R. G. (1985). The development of multiple personality disorder: Predisposing, precipitating, and perpetuating factors. In R. P. Kluft (Ed.), *Childhood Antecedents of Multiple Personality* (pp. 37-64). Washington, DC: American Psychiatric Press.

Brende, J. O. (1987). Dissociative disorders in Vietnam and combat veterans. *Journal of Contemporary Psychotherapy, 17,* 77-86.

Briere, J. (1989). *Therapy for Adults Molested as Children: Beyond Survival.* New York: Springer.

Caul, D. (1978, May). *Hypnotherapy in the Treatment of Multiple Personalities.* Paper presented at American Psychiatric Association, Atlanta, GA.

Caul, D. (1984). Group and videotape techniques for multiple personality disorder. *Psychiatric Annals, 14,* 43-50.

Caul, D. (1988). Determining the prognosis in the treatment of multiple personality disorder. *Dissociation, 1*(2), 24-26.

Caul, D., Sachs, R. G., & Braun, B. G. (1986). Group therapy in treatment of multiple personality. In B. G. Braun (Ed.), *Treatment of Multiple Personality Disorder* (pp. 143-156). Washington, DC: American Psychiatric Press.

Chase, T. (1987). *When Rabbit Howls.* New York: Dutton.

Chu, J. A. (1988). Some aspect of resistance in the treatment of multiple personality disorder. *Dissociation, 1*(2), 34-38.

Comstock, C. M. (1985, October). *Internal Self Helpers or Centers.* Paper presented at Second International Conference on Multiple Personality and Dissociative States, Chicago, IL.

Comstock, C. M. (1986, September). *The Therapeutic Utilization of Abreactive Experiences in the Treatment of Multiple Personality Disorder.* Paper presented at Third International Conference on Multiple Personality and Dissociative States, Chicago, IL.

Comstock, C. M. (1988, October). *Complications in Abreactions During Treatment of Multiple Personality and Dissociation*. Paper presented at Fifth International Conference on Multiple Personality and Dissociative States, Chicago, IL.

Coons, P. M. (1984). The differential diagnosis of multiple personality: A comprehensive review. *Psychiatric Clinics of North America, 7,* 51-67.

Coons, P. M. (1985). Children of parents with multiple personality disorder. In R. P. Kluft (Ed.), *Childhood Antecedents of Multiple Personality* (pp. 151-166). Washington, DC: American Psychiatric Press.

Coons, P. M. (1986). Treatment progress in 20 patients with multiple personality disorder. *Journal of Nervous and Mental Disease, 174,* 715-721.

Coons, P. M., & Bradley, K. (1985). Group psychotherapy with multiple personality patients. *Journal of Nervous and Mental Disease, 173,* 515-521.

Coons, P. M., & Milstein, V. (1984). Rape and post-traumatic stress in multiple personality. *Psychological Reports, 55,* 839-845.

Coons, P. M., & Sterne, A. A. (1986). Initial and follow-up psychological testing on a group of patients with MPD. *Psychological Reports, 58,* 43-49.

Courtois, C. A. (1988). *Healing the Incest Wound.* New York: Norton.

Crabtree, A. (1986). Explanations of dissociation in the first half of the Twentieth Century. In J. M. Quen (Ed.), *Split Minds/Split Brains: Historical and Current Perspectives* (pp. 85-108). New York: New York University Press.

Ellenberger, H. F. (1970). *The Discovery of the Unconsciousness.* New York: Basic Books.

Fagan, J., & McMahon, P. P. (1984). Incipient multiple personality in childhood: Four cases. *Journal of Nervous and Mental Disease, 172,* 26-36.

Fuhrman, N. L. (1988). Art, interpretation, and multiple personality disorder. *Dissociation, 1*(4), 33-40.

Goodwin, J. (1985). Credibility problems in multiple personality disorder patients and abused children. In R. P. Kluft (Ed.), *Childhood Antecedents of Multiple Personality* (pp. 1-19). Washington, DC: American Psychiatric Press.

Greaves, G. B. (1980). Multiple personality: 165 years after Mary Reynolds. *Journal of Nervous and Mental Disease, 16,* 577-596.

Greaves, G. B. (1988). Common errors in the treatment of multiple personality disorder. *Dissociation, 1*(1), 61-66.

Greaves, G. B. (1989). Precursors of integration in multiple personality disorder. *Dissociation, 2,* 224-230.

Grove, D. (unpublished). Workshop information available from David Grove Seminars, 20 Kettle River Drive, Edwardsville, IL 62025.

Herman, J. L., & van der Kolk, B. A. (1987). Traumatic antecedents of borderline personality disorder. In B. A. van der Kolk (Ed.), *Psychological Trauma* (pp. 111-126). Washington, DC: American Psychiatric Press.

Hilgard, E. (1977). *Divided Consciousness: Multiple Controls in Human Thought and Action.* New York: Wiley.

Hilgard, J. R. (1970). *Personality and Hypnosis.* Chicago: University of Chicago Press.

Horevitz, R. P. (1983). Hypnosis for multiple personality disorder: A framework for beginning. *American Journal of Clinical Hypnosis, 26,* 138-145.

Horevitz, R. P., & Braun, B. G. (1984). Are multiple personalities borderline? *Psychiatric Clinics of North America, 7,* 69-88.

Horowitz, M. J. (1987). *States of Mind: Configurational Analysis of Individual Psychology* (2nd ed.). New York: Plenum.

Horowitz, M. J. (1988). *Introduction to Psychodynamics.* New York: Basic Books.

Kaufman, G. (1985). *Shame: The Power of Caring* (2nd ed. rev.). Cambridge, MA: Schenkman.

Kemp, K., Gilbertson, A. D., & Torem, M. (1988). The differential diagnosis of multiple personality disorder from borderline personality disorder. *Dissociation, 1*(4), 41-46.

Kernberg, O. (1966). Structural derivatives of object relationships. *International Journal of Psycho-Analysis, 47,* 236-253.

Kluft, R. P. (1982). Varieties of hypnotic interventions in the treatment of multiple personality. *American Journal of Clinical Hypnosis, 24,* 230-240.

Kluft, R. P. (1983). Hypnotherapeutic crisis intervention in multiple personality. *American Journal of Clinical Hypnosis, 26,* 73-83.

Kluft, R. P. (1984a). Treatment of multiple personality disorder. *Psychiatric Clinics of North America, 7,* 9-29.

Kluft, R. P. (1984b). Multiple personality in childhood. *Psychiatric Clinics of North America, 7,* 121-134.

Kluft, R. P. (1984c). Aspects of the treatment of multiple personality disorder. *Psychiatric Annals, 14,* 51-55.

Kluft, R. P. (Ed.). (1985a). *Childhood Antecedents of Multiple Personality.* Washington, DC: American Psychiatric Press.

Kluft, R. P. (1985b). The natural history of multiple personality disorder. In R. P. Kluft (Ed.), *Childhood Antecedents of Multiple Personality* (pp. 197-238). Washington, DC: American Psychiatric Press.

Kluft, R. P. (1985c). Childhood multiple personality disorder: Predictors, clinical findings, and treatment result. In R. P. Kluft (Ed.), *Childhood Antecedents of Multiple Personality* (pp. 168-196). Washington, DC: American Psychiatric Press.

Kluft, R. P. (1986a). Personality unification in multiple personality disorder. A follow-up study. In B. G. Braun (Ed.), *Treatment of Multiple Personality Disorder* (pp. 29-60). Washington, DC: American Psychiatric Press.

Kluft, R. P. (1986b). Treating children who have multiple personality disorder. In B. G. Braun (Ed.), *Treatment of Multiple Personality Disorder* (pp. 79-106). Washington, DC: American Psychiatric Press.

Kluft, R. P. (1987a). An update on multiple personality disorder. *Hospital and Community Psychiatry, 38,* 363-373.

Kluft, R. P. (1987b). The simulation and dissimulation of multiple personality disorder. *American Journal of Clinical Hypnosis, 30,* 104-118.

Kluft, R. P. (1988a). The phenomenology and treatment of extremely complex multiple personality disorder. *Dissociation, 1*(4), 47-58.

Kluft, R. P. (1988b). The postunification treatment of multiple personality disorder: First findings. *American Journal of Psychotherapy, 42,* 212-228.

Kluft, R. P. (1988c). On treating the older patient with multiple personality disorder: "Race against time" or "make haste slowly"? *American Journal of Clinical Hypnosis, 30,* 257-266.

Kluft, R. P. (1989a, April). On optimism in the treatment of MPD: A status report by a participant observer. *Trauma and Recovery.* (A newsletter of the Ohio Society for the Study of Multiple Personality and Dissociation; Appendix, pp. 85-86.)

Kluft, R. P. (1989b). Playing for time: Temporizing techniques in the treatment of multiple personality disorder. *American Journal of Clinical Hypnosis, 32,* 90-98.

Kluft, R. P. (1989c). The rehabilitation of therapists over-whelmed by their work with multiple personality disorder patients. *Dissociation, 2,* 243-249.

Kluft, R. P., Braun, B. G., & Sachs, R. (1985). Multiple personality, intrafamilial abuse, and family psychiatry. *International Journal of Family Psychiatry, 5,* 283-301.

Kohut, H. (1971). *The Analysis of the Self.* New York: International Universities Press.

LaCalle, T. M. (1987). *Voices.* New York: Dodd Mead.

Lovitt, R., & Lefkof, G. (1985). Understanding multiple personality with the Comprehensive Rorschach System. *Journal of Personality Assessment, 49,* 289-294.

Mayer, R. (1988). *Through Divided Minds: A Doctor's Exploration of Multiple Personalities.* New York: Doubleday.

Missildine, W. H. (1963). *Your Inner Child of the Past.* New York: Pocket Books.

Orne, M. T., Dinges, D. G., & Orne, E. C. (1984). On the differential diagnosis of multiple personality in the forensic context. *International Journal of Clinical and Experimental Hypnosis, 32,* 118-169.

Polster, E., & Polster, M. (1973). *Gestalt Therapy Integrated: Contours of Theory and Practice.* New York: Brunner/Mazel.

Prince, M. (1906). *Dissociation of a Personality.* New York: Longman, Green.

Putnam, F. W. (1984). The psychophysiologic investigation of multiple personality disorder: A review. *Psychiatric Clinics of North America, 7,* 31-39.

Putnam, F. W. (1989). *Diagnosis and Treatment of Multiple Personality Disorder.* New York: Guilford.

Putnam, F. W., Guroff, J. J., Silberman, E. K., Barban, L., & Post, R. M. (1986). The clinical phenomenology of multiple personality disorder: Review of 100 recent cases. *Journal of Clinical Psychiatry, 47,* 285-293.

Riley, K. C. (1988). Measurement of dissociation. *Journal of Nervous and Mental Disease, 176,* 449-450.

Ross, C. A. (1989). *Multiple Personality Disorder: Diagnosis, Clinical Features, and Treatment.* New York: Wiley.

Ross, C. A., & Anderson, G. (1988). Phenomenological overlap of multiple personality disorder and obsessive-compulsive disorder. *The Journal of Nervous and Mental Disease, 176,* 295-298.

Ross, C. A., & Gahan, P. (1988). Techniques in the treatment of multiple personality disorder. *American Journal of Psychotherapy, 42,* 40-52.

Rowan, J. (1990). *Subpersonalities: The People Inside Us.* New York: Routledge.

Sachs, R. G., Frischolz, J., & Wood, J. I. (1988). Marital and family therapy in the treatment of multiple personality disorder. *Journal of Marital Therapy, 14,* 249-259.

Sakheim, D. K., Hess, E. P., & Chivas, A. (1988). General principles for short-term inpatient work with multiple personality disorder patients. *Psychotherapy, 25,* 117-124.

Sanders, S. (1986). The perceptual alteration scale: A scale measuring dissociation. *American Journal of Clinical Hypnosis, 29,* 95-102.

Sidis, B., & Goodhart, S. P. (1905). *Multiple Personality: An Experimental Investigation into the Nature of Human Individuality.* New York: Appleton.

Solomon, R. S. (1983). Use of the MMPI with multiple personality patients. *Psychological Reports, 53,* 1004-1006.

Spiegel, D. (1984). Multiple personality as a post-traumatic stress disorder. *Psychiatric Clinics of North America, 7,* 101-110.

Spiegel, D. (1986). Dissociation, double-binds, and post-traumatic stress in multiple personality disorder. In B. G. Braun (Ed.), *Treatment of Multiple Personality Disorder* (pp. 61-78). Washington, DC: American Psychiatric Press.

Spiegel, D. (1989). Hypnosis in the treatment of victims of sexual abuse. *Psychiatric Clinics of North America, 12,* 295-305.

Spiegel, H. (1963). The dissociation-association continuum. *Journal of Nervous and Mental Disease, 136,* 374-378.

Strean, H. S. (1985). *Resolving Resistances in Psychotherapy.* New York: Wiley.

Summit, R. (1983). The child sexual abuse accommodation syndrome. *Child Abuse and Neglect, 7,* 177-193.

Taylor, W. S., & Martin, M. F. (1944). Multiple personality. *Journal of Abnormal and Social Psychology, 39,* 281-300.

Torem, M. (1986). Dissociative states presenting as an eating disorder. *American Journal of Clinical Hypnosis, 29,* 137-142.

van der Hart, O., & Friedman, B. (1989). A reader's guide to Pierre Janet on dissociation: A neglected intellectual heritage. *Dissociation, 2,* 3-16.

Wachtel, P. L. (Ed.). (1982). *Resistance: Psychodynamic and Behavioral Approaches*. New York: Plenum.

Wagner, E. E., Allison, R. B., & Wagner, C. F. (1983). Diagnosing multiple personalities with the Rorschach: A confirmation. *Journal of Personality Assessment, 47*, 143-149.

Watkins, H. H. (1980). The silent abreaction. *International Journal of Clinical and Experimental Hypnosis, 2*, 101-113.

Watkins, J. G. (1978). *The Therapeutic Self*. New York: Human Sciences Press.

Watkins, J. G. (1984). The Bianchi (L. A. Hillside Strangler) case: Sociopath or multiple personality? *International Journal of Clinical and Experimental Hypnosis, 32*, 67-101.

Watkins, J. G., & Watkins, H. H. (1979). Ego states and hidden observers. *Journal of Altered States of Consciousness, 5*, 3-18.

Watkins, J. G., & Watkins, H. H. (1981). Ego-state therapy. In R. J. Corsini (Ed.), *Handbook of Innovative Psychotherapies* (pp. 252-279). New York: Wiley.

Watkins, J. G., & Watkins, H. H. (1984). Hazards to the therapist in the treatment of multiple personalities. *Psychiatric Clinics of North America, 7*, 111-119.

Watkins, J. G., & Watkins, H. H. (1988). The management of malevolent ego states in multiple personality disorder. *Dissociation, 1*(1), 67-72.

Whitfield, C. L. (1987). *Healing the Child Within*. Deerfield Beach, FL: Health Communications. .

Wilbur, C. B. (1988). Multiple personality disorder and transference. *Dissociation, 1*(1), 73-76.

Young, W. C. (1986). Restraints in the treatment of a patient with multiple personality. *American Journal of Psychotherapy, 50*, 601-606.

Young, W. C. (1988a). Observations on fantasy in the formation of multiple personality disorder. *Dissociation, 1*(3), 13-20.

Young, W. C. (1988b). Psychodynamics and dissociation: All that switches is not split. *Dissociation, 1*(1), 33-38.

Young, W. C., Sachs, R. G., & Braun, B. G. (1988). *A New Clinical Syndrome: Patients Reporting Ritual Abuse in Childhood Satanic Cults*. Unpublished manuscript.

Some Of The Other Titles Available
From Professional Resource Press

Innovations in Clinical Practice: A Source Book - **10 Volumes**
   Hardbound edition (Vols. 3-10 only) per volume... $54.20
   Looseleaf binder edition (Vols. 1-10) per volume..................................... $59.20
Cognitive Therapy with Couples... $17.70
Maximizing Third-Party Reimbursement in Your Mental Health Practice................. $32.70
Who Speaks for the Children?
   The Handbook of Individual and Class Child Advocacy....................................... $43.70
Post-Traumatic Stress Disorder:
   Assessment, Differential Diagnosis, and Forensic Evaluation............................. $27.70
Clinical Evaluations of School-Aged Children: A Structured Approach to
   the Diagnosis of Child and Adolescent Mental Disorders.................................. $22.70
Stress Management Training: A Group Leader's Guide.. $14.70
Stress Management Workbook for Law Enforcement Officers................................... $08.70
Fifty Ways to Avoid Malpractice:
   A Guidebook for Mental Health Professionals... $17.70
Keeping Up the Good Work:
   A Practitioner's Guide to Mental Health Ethics.. $16.70
Think Straight! Feel Great! 21 Guides to Emotional Self-Control............................... $14.70
Computer-Assisted Psychological Evaluations:
   How to Create Testing Programs in BASIC... $22.70

Titles In Our Practitioner's Resource Series

Assessment and Treatment of Multiple Personality and Dissociative Disorders ● Clinical Guidelines for Involuntary Outpatient Treatment ● Cognitive Therapy for Personality Disorders: A Schema-Focused Approach ● Dealing with Anger Problems: Rational-Emotive Therapeutic Interventions ● Diagnosis and Treatment Selection for Anxiety Disorders ● Neuropsychological Evaluation of Head Injury ● Outpatient Treatment of Child Molesters ● Pre-Employment Screening for Psychopathology: A Guide to Professional Practice ● *Tarasoff* and Beyond: Legal and Clinical Considerations in the Treatment of Life-Endangering Patients ● What Every Therapist Should Know about AIDS
All books in this series are $11.70 each

All prices include shipping charges. Foreign orders call or write for shipping information. All orders from individuals and private institutions must be prepaid in full. Florida residents add 7%. Prices and availability subject to change without notice.

See Reverse Side For Ordering Information   ⟶

To Order

To order by mail, please send name, address, and telephone number, along with check or credit card information (card number and expiration date) to:

Professional Resource Press
PO Box 15560
Sarasota, FL 34277-1560

For fastest service
(VISA/MasterCard/American Express orders only)
CALL 1-813-366-7913 or FAX 1-813-366-7971

Would You Like To Be On Our Mailing List?

If so, please write, call, or fax the following information:

Name:_____

Address:_____

Address:_____

City/State/Zip:_____

To insure that we send you all appropriate mailings, please include your professional affiliation (e.g., psychologist, clinical social worker, marriage and family therapist, mental health counselor, school psychologist, psychiatrist, etc.).